MW01107435

SUCCESS STARTS EARLY!

How Parents Can Prepare Their Children For School & Life Success

by Stan Wonderley
syndicated columnist

Success Starts Early!
How Parents Can Prepare Their Children
for School & Life Success

Published by:

Blue Bird Publishing
2266 S. Dobson #275
Mesa AZ 85202
(602) 831-6063 FAX (602) 831-1829
Email: bluebird@bluebird1.com
Web Site: www.bluebird1.com

©1997 by Stan Wonderley
All rights reserved. Printed in the U.S.A.

ISBN 0-933025-54-8
$14.95

Library of Congress Cataloging in Publication Data

Wonderley, Stan, 1923-
  Success starts early! : how parents can prepare their
children for school & life success / by Stan Wonderley.
    p.   cm.
  Includes bibliographical references (p.   ).
  ISBN 0-933025-54-8
  1. Education--Parent participation. 2. Reading--
participation. 3. Motivation in education. 4. Child
development. 5. Child rearing. I. Title
LB1048.5.W65 1997
649'.68-dc21   97-3117
                                                      CIP

ABOUT THE AUTHOR

Stan Wonderley has been concerned with the education of children for nearly 50 years. He has been a teacher at elementary and graduate levels of education, as well as a curriculum director. Wonderley has developed innovative programs that have made a difference with kids, and has been invited to do teacher training on his methods internationally.

He is the writer of the newspaper column "KIDS ARE MY BUSINESS" that is published in more than 40 newspapers in 10 western states. The information in this book is from the most popular articles that have appeared in his column.

DEDICATION
To all those children that I learned from in
Coalinga, California and Lake County, Oregon.
To the teachers in Lake County that let me try
new approaches to teaching.
And especially to my wife, Ellen,
for putting up with a mess.

TABLE OF CONTENTS

SECTION ONE

SECTION TWO

SUCCESS STARTS EARLY!

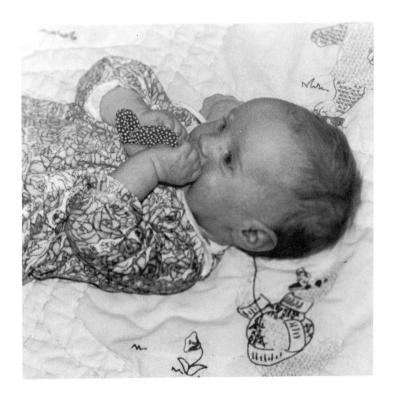

Childen do not have a fixed intelligence or a predetermined rate of intellectual growth. A child's level of intelligence can be changed by his home environment, especially in the first five years. Early stimulation will increase the chances of your child's success in academic and life skills. The most important thing you can do for your infant besides giving him love and security, is to read to him every day.

Photo by Lance Masterson
Courtesy of *Lake County Examiner*
Lakeview, Oregon

Section One

START EARLY—Building Academic Skills

> *Parental involvement is the number one factor in determining the success of a child's education.*
>
> **—Gary Bauer**
> **former U.S. Secretary of Education**

Chapter One

HOW TO INCREASE YOUR CHILD'S BRAIN POWER

While your child's body is growing rapidly during the first five years of life, what is happening to your child's brain?

Your child's intelligence is not fixed as was once thought. Yes, more than 50 percent of your child's intelligence is developed before he reaches school. What this really means is that parents have a larger, more important role in fostering the mental ability of their children. If you work toward increasing your child's intelligence long before the child goes to school, then he has a greater chance of success as a student and as a productive adult.

You, the parent, are the most important teacher your child will ever have. You have the opportunity to boost your child's intelligence. Teach your child individually at his own rate by those means with which your child is most likely to learn. Properly bonded with you, he will be a happier, healthier child and adult.

There are many success stories of parents using early learning techniques with their preschoolers. The major emphasis on early learning includes the following:

1. Children do not have a fixed intelligence or a predetermined

rate of intellectual growth. A child's level of intelligence can be changed by his home environment, especially during the first five years.

2. Early stimulation can and will produce changes in the size, structure, and chemical functioning of the brain.

3. It is accepted that heredity does put upper limits on a child's intelligence. However, this ceiling is so high that many researchers believe that no human has yet reached his potential intellectual capacity.

4. The changes in mental capacity are greatest during the period when the brain is growing rapidly. As the child grows older, the rate of physical growth and mental growth begin to decline. In other words, the child's capacity for intellectual development is greater the first year of life than it is during the fifth year of life.

5. Researchers believe that 50 percent of a child's intellectual development takes place during the first year of life, another 25 percent during the second year, and another 25 percent the rest of the person's life. In the first two years, the child has the greatest urge to learn. Dr. Bloom, a noted educator in the 1950s and 1960s, in his studies points out the importance of home environment to the intellectual development that has already taken place before the child enters school and the influence the home has during the elementary school years.

6. Scientists can tell us that the cortex of your child's brain can be roughly compared to a computer that must be programmed before it can operate effectively. During the first four years of life, the parent is helping to give the child's brain the sensory stimuli he sends to the brain through the child's eyes, ears, nose, mouth, and hands. The more sensory stimuli the child receives, thus activating the brain, the greater will be the capacity of the child's brain to function intelligently.

9

7. Children need to be introduced to computers by the age of three. Because of young children's unique capacity to learn, they can master computers at alarming rates if they are not pressured. All children can acquire a proficiency with programming that will become one of their more advanced intellectual accomplishments. Computers should not be considered an education gimmick or substitute but only a vehicle that the child's brain is capable of using to facilitate learning.

8. A baby is born with a built-in drive to learn that is equally as important as its need for food, water, and love. Babies want to explore, to investigate, and to experiment with their new world. The use of their senses—hearing, seeing, touching, tasting, smelling—satisfies their unique urge to learn. Parents should provide their child with the opportunity and a safe environment to experiment. Trying a multitude of sensory stimuli, children not only learn, but will be much happier. The baby who is dry, satisfied, comfortable, and still fussing in the crib or playpen has an unsatisfied basic need for new opportunities to learn. The child has a need for new sensory stimuli.

9. Essentially, it is the nature of young children to want to learn. They enjoy it and learn readily when their efforts are not overly controlled and pressured. They will need no awards, competition, punishment, or fear. Learning is a natural desire and is pleasurable for a young child. A good guide (parent) plans mentally-stimulating activities that are not too easy nor too difficult. The purpose of early learning activities is not to pressure, create competition, or show off but to make the young child happy.

10. The greater the variety of things the young child sees and hears, the more new things the child wants to experience. More new things to experience increases the child's ca-

pacity for coping with life later. Wise parents have the insight to match activities or stimuli in children's environment with their urge to learn and to provide challenges for the children. Too many parents underestimate the learning capacity of their child.

11. Music for the young child trains the brain for higher-level forms of thinking. Parents have known for a long time that music develops the child's intellectual powers and increases ability to do math and other reasoning skills. It was Plato in 1400 B.C. who said, "Music is a more potent instrument than any other for education." That is why some parents start their children in music lessons at three years of age. They also push for the school to include daily music for their primary-age children.

12. Daily exercise sends stimuli to the brain, feeding it nutrients in the form of glucose and increasing nerve connections which make it easier for young children to learn. Parents who take their youngsters out-of-doors to play and run vigorously is doing much for their children's intellectual development. Too many children spend their days inactively and are not in good physical condition. They need to go to a playground or park to run and play. It is natural for them to do this if given the opportunity.

13. Art is a great medium to foster the young child's intellect. Art educators have recognized the importance of young children experimenting with paints, crayons, scissors, and other art materials. Art experiences stimulate the brain for higher levels of thinking and develop the child's intellectual power.

STIMULATION: A NECESSITY FOR ANY BABY

During your baby's second six months of life, he is learning at a phenomenal rate.

Continue to give your baby the stimuli needed for intellectual development and provide opportunities to experiment. Your baby, for example, will pick up an object and drop it again and again. The baby is experimenting with the relationship of moving an object and dropping it on the floor.

Dr. Newell Kephart said, "In fact, the force of gravity is the one constant point around which a baby systematizes all the spatial relationships he or she is working out for itself during his or her early sensory-motor states of life."

Stimulate your baby's mental development with the following activities:

❋ Provide your baby with a variety of objects to touch, taste, throw, grasp, and shake. Be sure objects are safe. Bells, for example, are great stimulation. Floating animals, boats, and pouring utensils encourage babies to experiment with water in the bathtub. When your baby is going to sleep, have one or two cuddly, stuffed animals with interesting textures close by.

❋ As soon as your baby is able to crawl forward, he needs to be taken out of the playpen and placed on a clean floor where he can move along. Encourage crawling by putting toys just out of reach and cheering him on.

During the crawling stage, baby-proof your home by placing electrical cords out of reach and capping electrical outlets. Your baby should be free to explore and manipulate without being discouraged or frustrated with a bombardment of "don'ts."

Before your baby's twelfth month, he will utter his first words. Be excited! Encourage language development by naming objects the child is looking at or handling: "cup," "cookie," or "block."

❋ Put your actions into words by saying: "Now, we're putting on your shoes," and "Sit on my lap and I will rock you." Continue talking to your baby during his waking hours. When your baby babbles, be a good listener. Encourage other members of the family to converse. Babies are great listeners, and the information is being stored for later use.

Your baby will learn language correctly if you talk to him just as you would to an adult. Use complete sentences.

✳ Continue reading picture books to your baby. Get books with large pictures and point out objects such as houses, trees, etc. Let your baby help turn the pages. Your bookstore will have the right books for your child.

Do not worry about whether your child is understanding what you are reading. Children need the cuddling, the sound of their parent's soothing voice, and the rich language found in children's literature.

✳ Provide lots of opportunities for your baby to drop things, throw objects, pick up and release, poke, push, and pull. Yes, bang small pots and pans. During this second six months, your baby will be more serious about the results of his experimenting with objects. Your baby will be thrilled by grasping objects with thumb and fingers. Notice that he will pursue crumbs on the high chair tray while eating.

✳ Continue to sing lullabies and have easy-listening music on to lull your baby to sleep. Babies do respond to a singing voice. Your baby doesn't care whether or not you can carry a tune. Music has a way of developing auditory discrimination and memory, which your child will use later when learning to read. The amount of sensory stimuli and muscle activity your baby experiences the first six months of life will be reflected in his learning behavior. The more stimuli, the greater the capacity for learning your child will exhibit later in life.

DON'T DELAY; LEARNING BEGINS IMMEDIATELY

Children are ready and eager to learn the day they are born. In fact, over the first six months of a child's life, his learning rate is phenomenal. Enormous amounts of sensory stimulation are needed to give your baby's brain the information it needs to function and form concepts.

During this time, the brain is most receptive to receiving and recording sensory experiences. So, if you want to raise a healthy, happy, and bright child, these are some of the things you should be prepared to do:

❋ The day your baby is born, she is ready to be read to. Read whatever interests you—picture books, riddle books, Mother Goose books, etc. Read every day or as much as you want. If you have older children, encourage them to read to your newborn baby. Reading is the most calming thing you can do for your child. *The Real Mother Goose* is a good book with which to start. You can check it out at the library.

❋ Talk to your baby while she is nursing and while you are changing diapers. Yes, talk to your child all the time. Encourage older siblings to talk to the baby as well. Babies are born with an amazing listening capacity. Listening to you talk is how language is learned.

❋ For the crib, provide objects that can be seen, touched, moved, and experienced by the baby. Through these sensory experiences, your baby learns about the world around her. Above the crib, place an interesting mobile that can be watched. Put a nonbreakable mirror in the crib, so your baby can fool around with it as well.

❋ Listening to classical music is another experience to which your baby will respond and learn. Your baby will pick up on the melody and rhythm and will calm down and enjoy listening to the music.

In order to encourage bonding between your and your baby, you must cuddle her at every opportunity. A child has a great need to have a strong bond with his parents. Not only does bonding help develop a secure and happy child, it is essential for future behavior and attitudes.

❋ Take your baby for walks. Your baby will enjoy seeing houses, trees, birds, and other people. Sounds are also important. Call attention to birds chirping and cars going by. It really doesn't matter what you talk about, as long as you talk to your baby. Remember, the child has an amazing listening capacity, a skill he will use daily during the years of formal education.

❋ Sing lullabies of years gone by. Especially effective is a solo by Dad. A baby responds to the singing voice, helping her develop auditory discrimination—listening and rhythm skills, which are all needed when it comes time to learn to read. Also, this activity develops a child's capacity for learning. Your soothing voice will lull your baby to sleep.

❋ As soon as your baby is able to crawl, place objects such as old pots or blocks of wood on the kitchen floor to encourage your baby's sense of adventure. These activities develop hand-eye coordination so necessary later for drawing and writing.

❋ It is critical for parents to develop a loving, personal relationship in which parent and the child learn from each other and shape each other's behavior. Your baby learns by discovering how to please you and how to fit into the environment you have created for her. The more nurturing you provide, the stronger the bond between parent and child.

MOST CRITICAL TIMES COME WHEN CHILD IS FROM ONE TO THREE

The years between one and three are the most critical two years in your child's life. During this time period, your child:

✏ learns the language of his parents.
✏ develops enough body control to walk, climb, jump, run, and manipulate objects.
✏ begins to question, joke, demand, and seek help.
✏ will show signs of his own learning style.
✏ begins to form personality based on innate temperament and heredity, as influenced by environment.

A child's home environment and his relationship with their parents are essential during these two years. Researchers estimate that only 10 percent of all families give their children optimum opportunities for developing their intellect. Very likely, these are the same 10 percent of kids that are named to future honor rolls.

Raising bright children takes time, energy, and dedication. If raising an intelligent child is your goal, remember the following:

✏ Freedom to explore their environment and help in learning the language is essential. Talk to your child, using complete sentences.
✏ A person's approach to life is determined by his parents' actions during these critical years. Remember this when providing direct and indirect modeling.

Design a physical environment suited to nurturing a child's natural curiosity by providing safe objects to play with

16

and opportunities to move about freely.

Teach your toddler the meaning of "no." Use the following technique to get your point across. Sit down in front of your child and hold the child securely by the forearms with the child's hands pressed against his cheeks. Look directly at the child's face and firmly say "no" and "don't touch that." Then let the toddler loose and give him a hug. This method will compel a child to pay attention.

Talk to your toddler. Talk while you are preparing dinner, vacuuming, dining, going to the grocery store, working in the yard or on the car. Talk about everything. The more you talk, the richer the child's vocabulary will become. Continue to talk, and by the end of the child's second year, you will not be able to count all the words he knows.

As your two-year-old improves his vocabulary, begin playing word games. For example, "I'm thinking of something that is red and is in this room. What is it?" Another game is to strike a glass of water with a spoon or jangle keys on a chain and then ask what made the sound. This may be too advanced for most two-year-olds, however.

Remember the importance of reading. Your child will gain great pleasure from your reading picture books. A good time for this is right before your child goes to sleep, but this should not be the only time. At this age, your child will probably enjoy reading each day. Also, be sure your child sees you reading for adult information and pleasure.

We should not call them the "Terrible Twos." Instead, appreciate your child's need to learn. Appreciate it and help foster it with positive encouragement. Enjoy your child's growing ability to run, climb, question, and chatter.

If you give your youngster the opportunity to learn, then he will be much easier to live with. When parents suppress learning, this age can truly become terrible.

Effective parents share several traits. They seem to be

people with high levels of energy; they had at least one teaching parent; and they have strong bonds with their own parents.

STIMULATING INTELLECTUAL GROWTH - AGES TWO TO FOUR

Most parents want to boost their child's mental ability so the child will be confident and successful when starting school. At this age, children's minds work so fast and reach out in so many directions that they many miss out on learning opportunities. One of the greatest opportunities of preschool learning at home is your ability to adapt to the immediate needs of your child.

The following activities help stimulate intellectual growth for preschoolers:

✎ At this age, your child's vocabulary growth is explosive and is largely learned from you. Speak correct English and, at the end of five years, your child will be expressing his feelings properly.

✎ Your child will discover, with very little effort, how to form tenses, plurals, and clauses without assistance from you. All you have to do is provide the correct example. Your child's ability to form correct speech patterns is greater now than it will ever be again.

✎ Children love huge words and will enjoy saying them, especially if they know what they mean. They love, for example, to say dinosaur names, such as "brontosaurus," or car parts, such as "carburetor." Libraries have great books on both these subjects.

✎ Almost all three to five-year-olds go through a stuttering stage or, as one four-year-old said to his father, "I don't have enough words for my thoughts." Relax. The stuttering will go away. Don't call attention to the affliction; just keep talking and listening to your child.

✎ Use precise words. In describing a cloud, you might say, "The cloud is big and fluffy and looks like it might bring some rain." Use a similar strategy in describing cars, trucks, flowers, etc.

✎ Make it a daily practice to give your preschooler your undivided attention. One way to achieve this is to listen with the same respect you usually reserve for another adult. Then, your child will not be tempted to rush through what he wants to say. This courtesy will also increase your child's self-confidence, while reducing his need to whine for attention.

✎ During this age, use language to encourage thinking and planning ahead. "After you help me put away the dishes, we can read a story together." "Should we make cookies or go for a walk to the playground?" "If you move your glass of milk to the center of the table, you won't knock it over with your elbow."

✎ Language requires thinking. Begin asking questions, such as, "How many eggs can you hold in one hand?" "What is the difference between chewing gum and candy?" Or, "How do we know how fast a car is traveling?"

✎ The most important activity you can do for your preschooler is to read books daily for at least 15 minutes, or as often as your child's attention span allows. Reading to your child develops listening skills and left-to-right eye movement; enriches vocabulary; increases general knowledge (and love of books and reading), auditory discrimination, imagination, and expressive oral language; promotes parent/child bonding; and increases your child's intellectual growth. Remember, children enjoy listening to slightly complex texts with good rhymes and effective word repetition.

19

✎ Television can be turned into a stimulus for your child's vocabulary development, especially if you encourage your child to discuss the program. This gives you an excellent opportunity to sort out fact from fiction and clear up any misunderstanding your preschooler may have. No child should watch more than two hours of TV per day.

✎ Provide plenty of art materials for your preschoolers to create. Appreciate the effort, if not the content. Basic supplies include white paper, crayons, blunt scissors, paint, brushes, and school glue. Provide a drawer or box in which to store the supplies when your child is through. This teaches responsibility.

✎ Your library has many children's books that are just right for you and your child. Visiting the children's section should become a regular routine. Your child's intellectual growth is the greatest during the preschool years. Don't leave these important, informative years up to someone else or to chance. If your child starts to school poorly prepared, he will never catch up with those who are better prepared.

PLAY FOR PRESCHOOLERS DEVELOPS IMPORTANT SKILLS

When preschoolers are actively playing, they are developing many skills that are reading related. You should make an effort to limit TV viewing for your preschooler, because TV viewing is not playing. Play helps develop many skills that are reading-related.

Some good examples of active play include building a city with blocks or other materials; playing in the dirt with a toy truck; pretending to build a road; using modeling clay to make all kinds of creatures; dressing a doll and playing house. All of these activities develop small and large muscles, as well as thinking skills, which are important reading-related skills. The following ideas will help you get started:

🖎 Putting puzzles together. When preschoolers put a puzzle together, they are developing skills in seeing different shapes, which will be needed to distinguish between similarly shaped letters and words that look alike, such as "g" and "q," "m" and "n," and "look" and "book."

🖎 Building with blocks. When preschoolers are building with blocks and logs, they are developing position word concepts such as under, on top, bigger, behind, beside, and over. Also, preschoolers will be better able to follow directions, such as "put the books beside the lamp on the table."

🖎 Pretending and using imagination. When your preschooler is pretending to be another character such as a police officer, fire fighter, mother, or daddy, these creative play activities help them develop oral language skills and imagination, which will help them understand what they will read later.

🖎 Limit TV viewing. Limit the amount of time your preschooler spends in front of a TV. Viewing TV is a passive experience, and learning to read requires that the child be aggressive enough to make the effort it takes to learn to read. Learning to read can be very difficult if your child lacks the basic learning skills needed for later reading success.

When you give your preschooler plenty of opportunities to play with a variety of materials, he learns from these creative experiences and discovery. All you need to do is ask questions, give suggestions, praise your preschooler, then admire what he is able to do and learn.

SUCCESS STARTS EARLY!

CHARACTERISTICS OF A BRIGHT CHILD

Most parents can raise the intellectual level of their children by providing a stimulating, warm home environment. Children may be born with a poor, average, or superior brain, but an enriched home environment will raise a child's level of intelligence, regardless of the gene the child has inherited. If, for example, your child is born with an average brain at birth, chances are great that a warm, loving, mentally-stimulating environment from the day the child is born will help him develop into a bright or even a gifted youngster.

Homes that are stimulating in early childhood have played a part in the lives of a high percentage of very bright and highly-gifted individuals who are high-achievers. When researchers investigate into the background of school-age children rated as gifted by I.Q. tests, they find a stimulating home life and often deliberate planning by parents to help their children learn to use their brains.

Researchers at the University of Chicago reported that "Boys and girls who are mentally superior have become so because of (1) a home and school environment which stimulated them to learn and to enjoy learning; (2) parents and other significant persons who set examples of interest and attainment in education which the children unconsciously imitated; and (3) early family training which produces a desire for achievement in the child."[1] When these influences act upon a child with average or better biological equipment for learning, the child will probably become mentally superior.

Researchers point out that if a child is born with high biological endowment and does not receive adequate early stimulation, the child will not develop into a bright or gifted child. It has been pointed out that about one-half of potential

[1] Havighurst, Robert J. "Conditions Productive of Superior Children." *Teachers College Record, Vol 62.* April 1962.

gifted children are wasted for lack of early opportunities to learn at a sufficiently rapid rate and an enriched environment that promotes intellectual development.

Bright children have the following characteristics:

- ✍ Fewer emotional problems: They have fewer emotional problems and are better able to cope with the few problems they may encounter. They are more emotionally stable and more mature emotionally than their classmates.
- ✍ Learn faster: They learn much faster and easier than other youngsters and may learn in different ways than their classmates. Frequently, they do not need the step-by-step learning process that other children need; rather, they acquire information in great jumps. (Occasionally, these children become bored with the traditional classroom instruction.)
- ✍ Popular with classmates: They are usually well-liked and popular with their classmates and children of all ability levels. They are frequently elected to school offices and hold more leadership posts in extracurricular activities than their classmates. They do well on psychologists' tests. They usually have many friends.
- ✍ Have wide interests: They participate in sports and other activities and clubs. They have more hobbies and wider interests. They collect more things; they are more scientific. They learn more games than their classmates. Their writing skills are high and tend to reveal greater insight. They also are able to amuse themselves when friends are not around.
- ✍ Good sense of humor: They have a more active sense of humor. They tend to appreciate jokes and enjoy telling them. They are rated as happier and more enthusiastic in general than other children.
- ✍ Good physical coordination: As a group, they tend to be

better physically coordinated and have better physical endurance. They seem to have fewer illnesses and above-average general health.

✍ Self-critical: They seem to underestimate their abilities and accomplishments. They brag less than other children. They are more self-critical. They may tend to rate the achievements and abilities of average classmates higher than their own achievements and abilities.

✍ Music and art: As a general rule, they do better in music and art. They score high on measurements of creativity and originality.

✍ Fewer behavior problems: Generally, they cause fewer problems for their parents. They are more self-sufficient and self-directed. They are less likely to have undesirable personality traits. They are dependable self-starters and can adjust to problems and stress. They are responsible, conscientious, truthful, and trustworthy. They tend to cheat less in school and cause fewer discipline problems in school.

✍ Social conscience: They tend to have an active social conscience. They have a keen sense of personal responsibility and feel disturbed about injustices to classmates. They will play competitive games according to the rules, will stand up for the underdog, and have a keen awareness of the feelings and emotions of others.

✍ Common sense: They are able to apply what they know to new situations and, in seeing relationships, are able to use common sense to solve problems and reach a goal. They are especially good at finding positives in a person or situation.

✍ Likes school: They generally like school, unless they are pressured to conform to limited levels of work. Since they learn quickly without much repetition, they make good grades and will list difficult subjects as their favorites because of the challenges. They will read 50 percent more books than average students.

- ✍ Go to college: They are more apt to go to college and make better grades than their classmates. They will probably be on the dean's list. They are more apt to take post-graduate classes.

- ✍ Fulfill promises: When they become adults, they will fulfill the promise of their childhood and will become productive, happy, contributing, gifted individuals.

- ✍ High-level occupations: They will pursue high-level occupations, requiring leadership and higher level thinking skills. During their middle-age years, they will earn and achieve much more. As adults, they will read widely, especially biographies, history, and current events. They will participate in community affairs and run for public offices. They will enjoy a wide variety of sports. They will be superior physically and have better health.

- ✍ Are stable and predictable: They tend to have better marriages. They are stable and predictable, and their lives seem to be happy to a greater degree than do individuals of average intelligence.

Bright children are now thought to be a national treasure, to be cherished and helped to flourish.

Chapter Two

CREATIVE ARTS AND THE INTELLECTUAL DEVELOPMENT OF THE CHILD

Training in the arts creates better students. We do know that when children receive training in music, art, and creative dramatics, they tend to be the top students in our schools. In fact, they tend to be successful at all levels as students and adults. The fine arts have a way of giving all of us pleasure, building our self-confidence, and helping us to become better human beings.

Children need left-brain and right-brain activities. In the left brain, we process information in linear (logical sequencing), analytical (classifying), and quantitative (measuring) ways. Those things we can easily measure, such as reading, mathematics, and spelling are also directly controlled and developed by the left brain.

In the right brain, we learn to be creative in areas such as music, the visual arts, and creative dramatics. To be a well-rounded individual, both sides of the brain need to be developed.

It has been demonstrated that when we educate both sides of the brain, we are giving a child a two-thirds greater capacity for learning, as shown in the following illustration. It is important that parents do not neglect right-brain activities.

Art education is frequently neglected, misunderstood, or thought of as a "frill." However, several basic skills are developed in a child through art instruction. They include following four and five-step directions, developing critical listening skills, learning to plan and follow through on plans, developing problem-solving skills, developing visual perception, improving hand-eye coordination, creating new ideas, and thinking creatively.

Artist Sandy Campbell tells us that art education provides students with the needed observational tools to examine and discuss art forms of their own culture and other cultures and to better interpret art in history. Art also equips students with an appreciation for self-discovery and provides knowledge, skills, and attitudes which will encourage them to integrate art into their lives and their community. "In today's visually-oriented world, a student will find an extremely beneficial skill in art education," Campbell says. "Art gives students an appreciation for art form and design, which are essential in such fields as architecture, advertising, and engineering."

Incidentally, there are 87 careers requiring knowledge and skills in art. Don't knock quality art education. At your next parent-teacher conference, ask about the school's art program. If you have a special talent in art, talk to your child's teacher about sharing your talent with the class.

CREATIVE WAYS TO TEACH CREATIVITY

Most children around the age of three have an enormous amount of curiosity. They love to experiment, to test limits of different situations. They ask questions, usually in a penetrating way in order to annoy their parents. They are also not satisfied with simple answers.

Creative children are sensitive to what they see, hear, touch, and experience. You'll notice this sensitivity in the pictures they draw, as they have a surprising understanding of other people and their problems. They insist upon using the precise word for an object, feeling, or color. They enjoy sharing these observations with parents or other adults. Creative children find it easy to generate new ideas. They give uncommon answers to questions and may offer unusual solutions to other problems. They invent uncommon uses for common objects. They are usually active and see the humor or funny side of things. Many creative children are playful and love to work with ideas and to invent things.

Here are some ideas for encouraging and increasing creative abilities in your child:

○ When talking with your child, listen seriously and foster enthusiasm whenever you can. Show enthusiasm when your child creates, builds with blocks, and tinkers with toys.

○ Make your child feel unique by commenting positively on his differences.

○ When appropriate, let your child plan her own activities. For example, a two-year-old can decide whether to have a picnic or eat indoors. Encourage four-year-olds to select their own play outfits.

○ Play games such as "How many ways can you use a pencil?" Ask how many uses there are for an empty milk carton, a paper cup, or an old tire. Be encouraging and accepting—not critical—about the responses.

○ Make your preschooler think by asking questions such as: "What could we make with some scrap lumber in the garage?" "If you owned a television station, what kind of programs would you put on?"

28

◉ Play "what if" games. "What if it never got dark?" "What if everything we touched turned to gold or candy or ice cream?"

◉ Encourage new experiences. Let your preschooler watch a carrot top grow in a glass dish. Also take time to watch the shadings of a sunset or ice cream melting at room temperature.

◉ Provide a place where your child can be alone and just fool around with different objects and materials. Always have art materials available. On a warm day, dig a hole in the ground and fill it with water. Add a large spoon, and you have a recipe for fun in the sun. Don't worry about a little dirt.

◉ Enrich a child's life by providing simple musical instruments, such as bells, rhythm sticks, drums from oatmeal boxes, triangles, and glasses filled to different levels with water. Get a tape recorder and let your child listen to music.

Adults can stifle creativity by laughing at a young child's ideas and by pushing off suggestions with a what-do-you-know-you're-just-a-kid attitude. Parents must appreciate their children's creativity. It's worth it.

VISITING THE ART MUSEUM

Visiting art museums can be an enjoyable experience for the entire family and can broaden your children's outlook on the world. When you take your children to art museums, teach them to take a closer look at paintings or sculptures with a critical eye.

★ Ask what details in the painting they especially like or that stand out. Which details are fascinating or strange to their everyday life? What colors stand out in the painting? Why do they think the artist chose the colors?

★ Teach your children to look closely at the painting and ask the following questions: How did the artist achieve the appearance shown? What pattern did the artist use? Did the artist use geometric lines and shapes in the art? How was the color applied—with brushes or with dabs of color?

★ Did the artist show movement or noise? Have your children close their eyes for a moment and think of noises they might associate with the painting.

★ What story could be told about this painting? Read the caption to your children. Did the date of the painting have an effect on the painting? Does the painting tell anything about the country or place where the artist lived? Ask your children if they could recreate the "story" or create a different "story" to go with the painting. How is this painting similar to or different from the real life that your children live? How is life in the painting different from the life we live?

★ Ask your children if the artist enjoyed creating the painting or was the artist trying to portray a serious topic?

★ When looking at portraits, ask your children to compare the person with people they know. What similarities do they see? What differences? How have the fashions and hair styles changed? What would the people in the painting look like if they were dressed as we are? Looking closely at the clothes, were the subjects wealthy or poor? Which details in the clothing give you a clue?

Art helps children think creatively. Helping children observe art—whether in the form of paintings or sculptures—helps develop important skills, such as observing, comparing, classifying, expressive oral language, and vocabulary.

As a result of your visit to an art museum, your children may want to experiment with art. All you need to do is to provide materials such as paper, paint, and space. Art can stimulate a child's imagination and allows a child a special freedom to express feelings and thoughts.

ENCOURAGING KIDS' ART

At about two years of age, expect your child to grab a crayon or pencil and move it across the page in zigzag motions. He will be intent and fascinated by the images he creates and by the movements of his arms and hands. This kind of "art" should be encouraged. At this age, he will even want to see if he can pick up the lines he made.

Most children will start scribbling between 16 months and 2 years old. All you need to do is to provide paper and crayons or a pencil. They will do the rest. Parents should show interest and give appropriate praise. This masterpiece might be taped on the refrigerator door at the child's eye-level for all to admire.

Researchers have found that this pattern of development is universal, that children in other countries and cultures and even in other centuries have demonstrated the same cycles in their drawings. However, children who are handicapped, mentally or physically, may deviate from these patterns of growth.

Parents should view children's art as an opportunity to increase their awareness of the basic steps in the development of their children's artistic ability. As children grow, they want to dabble in other mediums, such as painting with a brush, which takes more control, or fooling around with clay.

The following tips will encourage artistic growth and development:

31

★ Look at the child's drawing. Knowing the four stages in children's art will help you understand and appreciate the child's growth and development.

★ Ask questions and make specific comments about your child's art. "Looks like you are enjoying drawing." "I'm glad you are trying so many colors." "I see you made a lot of long lines." "Was it hard to make all those little dots?" Occasionally, it might be acceptable to say, "It's beautiful."

★ Show appreciation for your child's art. Displaying artwork is very important to the child. An especially nice piece of artwork might be framed.

★ Provide safe art materials and a place for children to work. The kitchen table is great. Kids can create while you get dinner.

★ Give opportunities for children to see fine art. When appropriate, take a trip to children's art museums in larger cities or art galleries in smaller towns.

★ Keep a collection of the child's art. Your child will be delighted with her early artwork in later years. Your child's art is a unique, tangible record of growth and development.

The following art materials are appropriate:

✔ Crayons - one year old and older—large crayon with bright colors.

✔ Felt markers - one year and older. Choose water-based, nontoxic markers.

✔ Oil pastels - two years and older. Get the brighter colors. Your child will enjoy drawing on the side walks.

✔ Finger painting - two years and older. Get tempera paint and mix with liquid starch and use slick shelving paper. Wet the paper down with a sponge. Children love the shapes they can make with their fingers and hands. Use dad's old shirt and put it on backwards.

✔ Collages - ages three and up. Children will need your supervision.

✔ Clay modeling - ages three and up. Fun for young children to experiment with.

✔ Water colors - ages three and up. Be sure to choose sets that have the primary colors. They love to mix and fool around with colors. An easel might be in order.

✔ Tempera paint - ages three and up. It can be purchased in powder form and mixed. The paint should be fairly thick. Four or five basic colors are all you need, plus a brush for each color. Use 12" x 18" newsprint.

CREATIVE DRAMATICS AND ITS BENEFITS

Of all the teaching techniques, creative dramatics is the most powerful. Drama is the act of crossing into the world of story. When children are involved in drama, they live as if the story were true by entertaining its imaginal reality. The story is a basic way of organizing the human experience, a creative way of understanding. Drama enables the child to discover the heart of the story through visual images. It causes children to journey inside the story, so that they reconstruct the story in sequence of action. Drama helps children make their thinking visible.

Drama helps children develop creative thinking skills. It improves comprehension of subject matter. It builds bridges between the author and the reader. It makes learning personal and enjoyable. Creative dramatics crosses all age levels and interests, from bright children to those with special needs.

The benefits of creative dramatics are many:

✧ Stimulates interest in reading literature.

✧ Helps children enjoy the experience of playwriting and creating.

✧ Helps children decide which scenes to eliminate and which materials to delete in the writing process.

✧ Provides opportunities for actively conveying meaning in situations that require reflective thought and language.

✧ Educates the mind, body, and heart. Since drama is so creative, it helps children who learn in different ways and at different rates.

✧ Involves meaningful practice of small and large muscle control (physical activity).

✧ Encourages imagination and aesthetic development.

✧ Allows learners to take risks and still feel safe in extending themselves physically, emotionally, and intellectually.

✧ Permits young actors to show with their voices and bodies how a character feels and responds in a given situation.

✧ Encourages students to work in a social situation and promotes cooperation among group members.

✧ Promotes self-confidence and self-esteem.

✧ Provides opportunities for the child to play out the world as they see it and enables them to develop a personal understanding and appreciation of various areas of the curriculum.

✧ Gives children a satisfying feeling of accomplishment, especially if they perform before their parents, other students, and the community.

✧ Improves communication skills and problem solving and integrates all areas of subject matter.

✧ Can involve the parents in helping to make costumes and props and in helping their children to learn parts.

Creative dramatics is the best way to teach in many situations, because it puts language to use in purposeful, practical and meaningful ways. The student learns to use words correctly in order to portray the characters carefully and accurately. As children play different roles, they have opportunities to use different expressions, create different moods, and speak as different characters.

Through creative dramatics, children learn to speak clearly and loudly. Drama automatically becomes involved in the process of development of better speaking and listening skills. It can lead to a positive attitude about performing arts in general.

Parents can involve preschoolers in dramatics in the following ways: Read a story such as *Caps for Sale*. Help your preschooler gather up all the hats in the family and sell them to family members and friends for a penny, as they come home. The child must understand that this is pretend and that the hats must be returned after the game. With a little imagination, you and your child can have fun recreating picture books.

You might get pencil and paper and be the writer, while your preschooler does the talking. Creative dramatics is a natural for three to five-year-olds. All you need to do is provide a few props, like your old clothes, and you'll have a performance. Make sure you are a good listener.

Creative dramatics develops the following creative skills: thinking skills, inventive creativity, cognitive thinking skills, expressive oral language, creative writing, social skills, empathy, value judgments, and intuition. It helps children relate inner understandings into concrete action. It is a holistic approach to academic learning, and it provides a feeling of surprise and fun for the learner. It helps children become aware of their own imagination. It integrates mental and physical activity. Children begin to develop a sense of trust and self-awareness.

MAKING MUSIC A PART OF CHILDREN'S LIVES

Children who are involved in musical activities, such as singing and playing musical instruments, are reaping important benefits. Here they are:

1. Enjoyment and appreciation of music.
   Children who are surrounded by all types of music, especially classical music, from birth are much more apt to continue that enjoyment into adult life and to continue to expand their musical knowledge and interest.
2. Emotional release.
   Being able to sing and play an instrument is an emotional expression which can help to improve an individual's state of mind. People who were "down" or mildly depressed have created some of our best folk songs as a release of their frustrations. Singing or playing can be an individual expression increasing self-image, or a group activity promoting communications with others and a feeling of security.
3. Listening training.
   Musical training improves auditory discrimination and listening skills, which are so essential for learning to read. Young children are required to discriminate between rhyming words and sounds in beginning reading. Boys, in particular, often have great difficulty learning to read. Throughout the elementary grades, they are asked to gain information through listening. Musical training is invaluable in improving listening skills.

Here's what you can do. Sing songs with your preschoolers—all the traditional songs of our culture, such as: "Mary Had a Little Lamb," "Twinkle, Twinkle Little Star," and "Three Blind Mice." Songs with a lot of repetition make

36

it easy for children to remember and accurately reproduce the melody patterns—"A Hunting We Will Go," "She'll Be Coming 'Round the Mountain," and "Down in the Meadow."

Children eight years and older are ready to learn songs for group singalongs. Camp songs and holiday songs are always favorites. As a primary teacher, I always enjoyed singing traditional holiday songs. If you enjoy songs, so will your kids. They really don't care if you're not a great singer. By the end of the school year, the kids in my class could sing better than I could. My poor singing did not bother them. However, I can remember one little girl saying, "Mr. Wonderley, you're off key."

Singing with your kids at all ages increases bonding, which is vital for their emotional health and development.

Learning to play a musical instrument will greatly enhance a child's education and increase his academic skills. Experienced piano teachers report that three years of age is a good time to begin. I know a mother of a four-year-old who had always wanted to play the piano, so she took lessons with her son. By the time her son was eight, they were playing duets at recitals. It was great for both of them. Encourage your child to practice daily. Do not push or use it as punishment. Remember, your encouragement and listening ear will keep him going.

One of the mistakes parents make in music lessons is investing a lot of money in the early years. Then when children reach about 13, they get involved in school activities and want to drop out. One father told his talented daughter, "You're too good at the piano. Drop something else." She's still taking piano in her third year of college.

Another wise parent told her talented 14-year-old who wanted to quit piano lessons, "Okay, you can quit piano lessons, but you get yourself a job and pay me back all the money I've already spent on lessons." This lad knew his mother would stand firm. When he graduated from high school and was getting ready to attend a university, he announced that he wanted to take the family's prized Chickering piano with him. Of course, his mother said, "No way! We'll rent a piano for you." That lad is still learning the piano.

These two young people can use their musical skills in many ways, including teaching others. I know a mother who is using her piano teaching skills to put her kids through college.

Expose your children to all kinds of music. Don't send them to concerts; take them. Take them to ballets, operas, and contemporary music recitals. These will all expand your children's musical background. Your local schools give concerts that are free, and it is good music. At home, listen to classical as well as contemporary music on the radio and stereo. Cable companies have music that provides a wide range of listening, from symphony to traditional blues. All you have to do is push a couple of buttons. Just contact your local cable company for details and cost.

By exposing your children to music, you are giving them an opportunity to lead a richer, fuller life and to learn in the process. So go out and EXPLORE THE WORLD OF MUSIC! Your children will be better students and live fuller lives.

Chapter Three

PARENTAL INVOLVEMENT
MEANS SCHOOL SUCCESS

As a parent, it is crucial to be involved in your child's education at every level, from birth through college. You have the right to help decide who will be your child's teacher. There needs to be a partnership between parents and the school. You'll want to make time to volunteer and help with homework. When parents and teachers share responsibility, the job of educating kids is made easier. If your children see you involved at school, they will get a strong message that learning and good behavior are important.

Children learn best if all their senses are involved in the learning process. Young students can work in a simulated grocery store, while some teachers will use what actors rely on: props, suspense, humor, and surprise to capture the students' interest. Find teachers who are creative and not afraid to take risks.

You can raise your child's school scores by:

1. Being an involved parent.
2. Communicating your concerns.
3. Being your child's best cheerleader.
4. Contributing opinions when school decisions are being

made.

5. Being a volunteer in your child's classroom.
6. Thinking of ways for your school and community to team up.

Many school districts offer open or fundamental education, and some will use advanced teaching strategies. High school parents can choose the school with the educational philosophy they feel is best for their children.

When you match your child with the right school, your child will have an edge on learning and enjoy his schooling. Within the school, there are some teachers with personalities that may not match your child's temperament. If your child's temperament and the teacher's clash, it might be wise to switch classes. That does not mean the teacher is a poor teacher. The best teachers may have problems with certain children. If you need to switch teachers, use some diplomacy. Teachers are human beings with feelings, too.

One parent told me, "If I had it to do over, I would have hocked and borrowed to pay for the best elementary and high school education possible for my kids and would not have worried so much about putting money away for college."

Giving a child the very best possible education in the early years fine-tunes the child's talents and makes him better prepared to make the most of college. If your child is motivated and has the ability, then college can be paid for through loans, grants, scholarships, and money earned by your child.

Once your child reaches school age, do not turn all the responsibility for your child's education over to the school.

In 1987, the National Research Council's Mathematical Science Education Board reported that one reason American children do so poorly in mathematics, and Japanese and Chinese do so well is that their parents become involved in their children's schoolwork, encouraging homework and paying for tutoring when necessary. In the United States, parents tend to leave their children's progress up to the school. **If you want your child to get the very best education possible, you must be involved in your child's school.**

When choosing the right school and teacher for your child, ask if the teaching staff holds regular meetings. Children do much better in a school where teachers have a chance to share ideas. Out of such sharing comes a unified approach to each child, rather than conflicting rules and expectations. It can produce a school experience kept fresh and stimulating. In some schools, the teaching staff is tied down to so much paperwork that they do not have time to exchange ideas.

Bear in mind that nursery school experience is not for every child. Some children are not ready for a school situation, regardless of age. As a parent, you will know if your child is ready for nursery school. If your child is forced to go to school each day, he may display regressive behavior, such as bed wetting, upset stomach, and crying. Some children are not ready for school at four years of age. Allow your child to stay home. Your child may be better off with a parent staying home. Don't mess up a child for a few luxuries that can be purchased later.

HIGH SCHOOL STUDENT SUCCESS DEPENDS ON PARENTS' ATTITUDES

Parents may be the reason high school students succeed or fail in school. Principal Scott MacCluer says: "Parents need to be very involved with their children's schooling. Parents establish attitudes toward school and learning that influence their children for the rest of their lives."

MacCluer said that every kid comes home and answers the question, "What happened at school?" with "Nothing."

"If nothing happened in seven hours, then I should be fired, along with the staff," MacCluer said. "The parent who refuses to show interest gives subtle messages that school is unimportant and that success in the classroom is meaningless."

Parents should get involved. Ask children to share their knowledge about the Civil War. Bounce off their vocabulary words, and find out what they learned in math.

"If students and parents apply this strategy," MacCluer said, "they can't help but have positive results."

MacCluer said that if parents get involved in their children's education, become a sounding board for them and a source of encouragement, school will be a positive, rewarding experience for the student.

During the high school years, MacCluer said, parents are going through a traumatizing time. Their children are growing up and about to leave home. But that shouldn't mean parents leave their children alone and show no interest in their education. This time is the most crucial time for parents to take an interest.

MAKING THE MOST OF PARENT-TEACHER CONFERENCES

The parent-teacher conference offers an opportunity for sharing information about your child. The best conferences result when both the parent and the teachers feel they have learned something about the child. To make the most of parent-teacher conferences, both parents should talk and prepare ahead of time. Discuss things like what you want to tell the teacher about your child—his special interests, for instance, or, how he feels about school or what he does after school. Ask your child what you might discuss with the teacher and what you should look at in the room.

When you get to the conference, be sure to arrive on time. The teacher will be prepared to tell you about your child's school work. Here are some questions you might want to ask:

☞ In what subject does my child do well?
☞ What does my child need in order to improve?
☞ Are there any special programs that could help my child?

Ask questions about any part of the school's programs that you have questions about (e.g., homework, recess, test results). Be sure to leave promptly when your conference time ends.

After you get home, take time to tell your child something positive the teacher said about him. Take notes and jot down any important points you want to share with a spouse who was unable to attend the conference. Be positive about your child's teacher and school programs.

IMPROVING LISTENING SKILLS THROUGH GUIDANCE AND PATIENCE

The sooner your child learns to really listen, the better student he will be. When training your child to listen, it's best to begin with his name. When you're sure you have your child's attention, give the direction once and only once.

Your directions might be, "John, I want you to put your book away and set the table." If he ignores you, go to him and calmly ask, "Do you remember what I asked you to do a moment ago?" If he admits he wasn't listening, explain in a serious voice that you expect him to do as he is asked the first time. When he is finished setting the table properly, praise him.

Your positive reinforcement will go much further in

teaching him to listen and respond than any negative consequences you enforce for his failure to do what you ask him to
do.

These activities will develop good listening skills.

✓ Read to your child regularly.

✓ Ask your child questions about the stories you read to him/
her. Encourage your child to tell you what the story was
about and remember important details. If this process
proves too difficult, discuss the story a page at a time and
gradually lengthen the number of pages covered.

✓ Once in a while, sit somewhere with your child, close your
eyes and see how many different sounds your child hears
and have him keep a record of the sounds. Examples of
sounds may be dogs barking, car horns, or birds singing
and chirping. Your child may want to draw a picture of
these sounds when the walk is over.

✓ Listen to and memorize songs and sing them together in the
car or while you're cooking or weeding the garden.

✓ Give your child a series of oral directions to follow such as,
"Walk to the door, turn around in a circle, and hop back to
the couch." Work up to as many actions as your child can
handle. Most directions given by teachers are three-step
directions.

✓ Hide an object in a room and clap to provide clues to help
him locate the object. Clap loudly as he moves toward it,
and softly as he moves away.

✓ Read numbers to your child in order. Start with two-number
sequences and increase as your child is ready.

✓ Say short sentences and ask your child to repeat them to you.
Take turns building longer, add-a-word sentences when
your child can repeat the shorter ones without too much
difficulty. These can be silly and are fun for the whole
family to build together on car trips or at a picnic.

44

✔ Say a word and have your child say a word that rhymes with it. (Example: gold-cold, fed-bed, etc.)

✔ Say words that are slightly different. (Example: hit and hat; bed and bad.)

✔ You can play a game where you say three words, two of which begin with the same sound. Ask your child to tell you which word begins with a different sound. Ask your child to tell you which word begins with a different sound than the other two. (Example: monkey, lemon, man.)

✔ Pretend you're going on a trip and each person adds a new object to the list of things being taken. For example, the first person might say, "I'm going on a trip and I'm taking a toothbrush." The second person would repeat the first sentence and add to it. "I'm going on a trip and I'm taking a toothbrush and a book."

✔ Play Simple Simon.

Auditory memory is defined as the ability to remember what we hear and to be able to describe something we hear. Generally, auditory memory problems are not caused by hearing loss. However, if your child is having problems with auditory memory, you should see the school speech therapist and have her hearing checked. This service is often free through the school.

The following activities will help your child overcome auditory memory difficulties. They will take only 5 or 10 minutes daily but will lead to improved school work, better grades, a happier child, and a rewarded parent.

❖ Ask your child to tell you what she saw on television or at school today. As your child tells you, write down what your child said.

❖ Ask your child to tell you how to play her favorite game or sport.

❖ Read a story to your child, and after every few sentences or paragraphs, stop and have your child tell you the general idea of what happened.

❖ Ask your child to tell you what she does at the beginning of school, after lunch, and at the end of the school day.

❖ Help your child remember beginning letter sounds by saying the letter "b." Then, have your child cut out and paste from newspapers or old magazines as many pictures as possible of objects beginning with the "b" sound. Example: Picture of bear or boat.

❖ Say three words (table, fun, fan) and have your child tell which word has a different beginning sound.

❖ Help your children hear rhyming words by having them clap when they hear a word that rhymes with *sun*. Now, say the words *stove, run, house.*

❖ Read a short list of words to your child. Ask how many words were in the list. Then read the list again and ask what words were in it. Start with words that are related in some way. Example: apples, oranges, bananas, peaches. Then begin to use unrelated words, such as table, car, tree, boat. Then try numbers (37, 42, 16, 21). At first make them simple enough to ensure success.

❖ Go over a short song or poem very slowly. Ask your child to repeat short phrases after you.

❖ If your child is interested in music, you might consider music lessons. Music develops auditory memory and many other learning skills. There are good music teachers who give lessons. Let your child choose the instrument she would like to learn to play.

❖ Play a game while traveling or walking, called "rhyming words." You say a word, and your child thinks of a word that rhymes with your word. Example: You say "fat"; the response might be "cat" or "rat."

If you want to be successful in working with your child on auditory memory, use praise, such as "I'm glad you tried so hard," "You are getting better," or "You got two correct." Avoid ridicule or anger, which will only add to the problem.

BRAINSTORMING; IMPORTANT THINKING SKILL

When you sit down with your child and toss around as many possible solutions to a problem as you can think of, you are brainstorming. Brainstorming is important because it is the first step in the process of creative problem-solving. As parents, you can do much to foster creativity in your children. Always try to encourage unusual ideas. Encourage your child to experiment with ideas without criticism. The creative thinking process helps children develop abilities to deal with problems and new situations they encounter.

Riding in the car, meals, bedtime, or any time you set aside to spend with your child are great times to begin encouraging creative thinking. You will awaken part of your child's brain that can prove to be a useful and enjoyable tool later on in life. Instead of performing tasks in the usual way, your child will learn to invent alternative methods of doing things. Children who see the advantage to flexibility won't be so apt to resist new concepts in math when they encounter them. They will be willing to consider alternatives in their stories, and creative writing skills are likely to improve.

People with the ability to think creatively have more control over their lives, more power to influence the lives of others with inventions or solutions to practical problems or emergency situations. Help your children gain that extra control over their lives, and expand their minds to see more than they might otherwise see.

Try some of these creative thinking activities:

•❖ When your young children use books to make tunnels for their cars or make a house from a large carton, show some excitement. Say, "What a neat idea!"

•❖ Encourage your children to make presents for people, ornaments for Christmas trees. Encourage your children to make their own Halloween costumes.

•❖ Instead of throwing away old boxes and containers, find and encourage others in your family to also find new uses for them.

•❖ Keep a "scrounge box" filled with scraps of fabric, wood, paper towel tubes, shoe boxes, ribbons, egg cartons, coffee cans, left-over wallpaper—just about anything you can think of. Invite your children to make new inventions. Decorate items, gifts or whatever they like. This is especially nice to have on a long, rainy day.

•❖ Ask a lot of "What if…" type questions. Example: "What if you went camping and forgot your toothbrush? Can you come up with other ways to brush your teeth?"

•❖ Pretend you suddenly find yourself in a difficult situation. Your children can help you imagine something specific. Try to think of all the good or positive things you can find in that situation. Encourage your children to look for possible solutions, ways in which they would get out of that situation.

•❖ Brainstorm about anything. What uses could you find for a Styrofoam cup besides drinking? For a fork besides eating? For a piece of paper besides writing? For a nickel besides spending as money? If it were to rain on the day you'd planned to have a picnic, what else could you do to have fun?

Creative problem-solving involves: fluency (creating lots of idea); flexibility (accepting the possibility of more than one answer to a problem or more than one use for an object);

originality (creating ideas which are unusual and different); and elaboration. When you take time to develop creative thinking with your children, you are helping them become happier and become better students.

HELPING CHILDREN TO THINK

Learning to think starts in the home, long before children start to school. Being able to think goes far beyond the basic learning skills and simple memorization. Learning to think starts at birth. Teaching your young child to think is really a simple task, but it starts in the home with the parents.

These simple easy-to-do ideas will help you get started:

- Problem-solving. Have your young child think of solutions to real or hypothetical problems. Example: What would we do if we missed the bus?
- Decision-making. Let your child help in decision-making and discuss factors influencing your child's decisions concerning money, time, or transportation. Example: Do we have enough time to bake a cake before dinner?
- Giving reasons. Give your child the opportunity to elaborate further than "I like" or "I don't like." Ask why they feel that way, or ask them to tell you more about their drawing or painting. Sometimes you might have to help your child find the right words. Example: I like bright colors.
- Guessing or estimating. Have your child guess how many of their friends are the same age as they are and how many are older or younger. Encourage your child to find the answer, and ask them how to find the answer.
- Comparing. Have your child plant two plants. Give one plant too much water a the other one too little water. Let your child compare the difference. You might want to

have a third plant and water it correctly. Have a discussion about the plants. Ask questions, like "What do your think happened to the plant you under-watered?"

∽ Observing and memory stretching. Ask your child to look around the room and name all the objects that start with the letter "b." For the younger child, ask what color each room in the house is painted.

∽ Classifying. Let your child help sort the laundry by color. He can sort other objects, too, such as smooth rocks and rough rocks. You can think of other ways your child can practice classifying.

∽ Organizing. Start a project. Have your child help you write down all the steps needed to do the project, including materials needed and procedures to follow, and then get started. Baking cookies is always fun. (If your child cannot write, then you do the writing, while your child does the talking.)

∽ Cause and effect. Discuss why certain things, like picking up roller skates or putting toys away, need to be done. Example: What would happen if you left your bicycle outside in the rain?

As you do these activities with your young child, you will gain practice, and your child will develop better thinking skills. As you read books together, try asking your child what she thinks might happen next in the story.

BACK-TO-SCHOOL ORGANIZATION

When your children start back to school after the summer vacation, organizing your family makes for a smooth beginning:

✳ Have a meeting with your children and decide with them

50

where books will be put and where day packs will go. Make sure items are put where they belong and decide where and when homework will be done, with the TV and stereo turned off. Now that your family has defined the areas and time, you can get the support of the other members of the family.

* Have a decorated folder in which each child can put the work they bring home—things like drawings, paintings, math papers, and tests. You can sit down with each child and go over the work completed at school. You'll also know what they are studying at school. Be sure to ask questions and appropriate praise. Avoid negative comments. Let each child know that you are proud of his accomplishments.

* When the children bring home artwork, hang it on the refrigerator so everyone can admire it. Also, you may consider framing and giving some of the better artwork to grandparents, other relatives, and special friends at Christmas. Children's efforts need to be appreciated.

* Show your children how to organize their closets. Show your children how to hang matching "outfits" that are appropriate for school. Help them match shirts and pants, or shirts and skirts, and hang them together. While you are showing them, tell them you expect this closet to be neat and organized. Unless you show them how to get organized, they will never become organized.

* Meet with your children and decide whether they should get dressed for school before breakfast. Will they do their homework as soon as they come home or after school? Decide what TV programs will be viewed. This will assure that things will get done. When homework is being done, make sure your children's friends know that there will be no phone calls. You will answer the phone and take

messages. Be sure you and the children stick to the schedule.

✳ Develop a system so you can deal with all of the outside obligations of each member, such as after-school sports, parents' club meetings, and all the other organizations that take your time and your children's time. Maybe you'll need to set priorities. You and your children don't need to join or take part in every organization. Sometimes your children need you more that that organization needs you. Avoid letting your children get too involved in outside obligations, so that they don't have time to spend with the family and pursue hobbies.

✳ You should consider a large calendar, so you can write important events on it. Encourage each family member to refer to it before making a commitment.

The time you spend now getting you and your family organized will save time, your family will run more smoothly, everyone will know what to expect, you'll be happier, and your children will feel more secure. After the first week of school, things should be less confusing, if you and your family develop a routine that works.

VISUAL MEMORY IS AN IMPORTANT SKILL

Question: My fourth grader has trouble remembering what he sees. It takes him a long time to copy from the board. What can I do?

Your fourth grader is not the only one with that problem. Some very successful adults have learned to adjust to the same problem. This is a problem with what educators call "visual-motor memory." Simply defined, visual-motor memory is the ability to copy or reproduce what is seen. For example, a student must copy an assignment or sentence from the chalkboard. The student copies letter for letter, instead of visually remembering complete words and phrases. The child soon becomes frustrated, because everyone else is finished, and she has only started. This is because the child must take the time to look up at each letter or number.

Many students develop poor attitudes and habits about school, which are hard to change. Now, what can you do about the visual-motor memory problem your child has? The following activities will help:

❖ On a sheet of paper, draw a straight line, a circle, a square, a triangle, and a diamond. Show them to your child for 30 seconds, cover up the designs, and have your child draw the designs from memory. (At first you might want to start with three designs to ensure success.)

❖ On a piece of paper, write 25 - 32 - 14. Expose for 15 or 20 seconds; have your child reproduce the numbers. Extend these as the memory develops, and you might want to lengthen the time to assure success at first. If your child got two out of three the first time, give praise for getting two correct. Say, "Let's try another one." Make these sessions short and sweet.

❖ Show your child the following objects for one minute: pencil, coin, shoestring, knife, book, bottle cap. Cover the objects and remove one. Take the cover off and have your child identify the object that was removed. You might want to make a game out of this by letting your child see how well you do. You might also keep score.

❖ Use toothpicks to make patterns: have your child reproduce that pattern from memory. Start with simple designs and gradually make them harder.

❖ As you travel down the road, play a game of writing the license plates of cars. At the end of the trip, see who got the most. The whole family can have fun doing this activity.

❖ Write a word on a piece of paper. Cover it up and have your child write the word from memory. Now, try three words, and have your child copy all three words.

❖ Have your child copy math problems, such as 324+221, after exposing it for 30 seconds. Do this until your child can get it copied after a five second exposure. Your child might want to do the problems. You can do subtraction problems. You can extend this activity as much as you want.

❖ Have two each of the following coins: penny, nickel, dime, quarter, half dollar. Expose them mixed up in a row. Cover them up and have your child reproduce the same order. You can make a game out of this activity. Kids enjoy beating their parents. You can use knives, forks, and spoons and make a pattern of five at first, then extend it to nine. Examples: Place in a row a knife, fork, spoon, fork, knife.

❖ Show your child how you want the table set for dinner. Cover your sample and have your child set the table using a plate, fork, knife, spoon, napkin, water glass, etc. Be sure your child gets a verbal reward for doing such a good job.

As you and your child do these activities together, you will notice gradual improvement. Be patient. Avoid scolding, as this will cause anxiety, and you and your child will be at odds with each other. Then you will not be able to work with him.

To evaluate or test your progress, have your child reproduce from memory the following series of letters: N, A, O, P, S, T. Expose them for five seconds and ask the child to write them on a piece of paper. The child should be able to reproduce five out of six. You have now helped your child develop an important learning skill for academic success. You just might notice your child getting homework done more quickly and liking school better.

TAKING TESTS

The difference between getting high grades and low grades is directly related to a student's ability to take a test well. If your child is preparing to take a test, there are several things you can do to help:

✔ When your child is studying at home, try to provide a quiet, pleasant place, where other members of the family will not disturb him.

✔ Help your child get organized by having materials available, such as pencils, paper, dictionary, and textbooks.

✔ Offer lots of encouragement and appropriate praise for getting organized and not waiting until the last minute. Help your child think positively, and help him to relax.

✔ Tell you child that real learning takes place when studying is spaced over a period of days or weeks. Cramming rarely produces good results.

✔ Talk to your child about the need to get a good night's sleep and be well-rested. Taking a test demands a lot of energy.

✔ A healthy body leads to a healthy, active mind, so be sure your child gets a well-rounded diet.

✔ Talk to your child about skimming the entire test before starting. He can better estimate how much time to spend on types of questions on the test.

✔ Frequently, students will waste valuable time on questions they can't answer. Encourage your child to concentrate on the easier ones first, which will help him relax and gain confidence later.

✔ When taking essay-type tests, it is always helpful to jot down phrases that relate to the answers. This will help write the answer later, and it will be easier to write from notes.

✔ If you can help relieve some of your child's anxiety, both the teacher and child will benefit. Once you help your child become a successful test taker, he is more apt to be a successful student.

It is always helpful to know in advance what your child is studying at school, so you can be supportive. Remember, the home is an extension of the school. The school needs the home, and the home needs the school.

Encourage your child to complete all assignments and do the lessons on time, as tests are based on assignments and what is learned in the classroom.

MOTIVATION

Frequently, the school has to deal with students who have poor motivation to do daily lessons and work up to their ability. One parent told me, "My son is bright, but he just doesn't care about school work or completing daily lessons."

The best study system in the world will not help your child if he is not interested in learning. The teacher can assign a chapter to read, but unless the student is motivated to read the material, the chapter will not be read.

The first steps in getting better grades and improving learning are to increase motivation and lengthen the time and attention given to an assignment. Parents can make a big difference. Here are some ideas for helping to improve your child's motivation:

❊ The next time your child brings home a written comment or report card, ask if he failed or got low marks. Listen carefully to your child's answers and try to understand his point of view. Then try to explain the teacher's point of view. Be sure to show interest in your child's school experience and take what he says seriously. Take time to review his school work and discuss ways that he can improve those grades and negative comments from the teacher. Writing down a strategy for improving grades will have the greatest impact. You might consider having both of you sign a simple contract or promise that is attainable.

❇ Occasionally, there are problems that the two of you need to deal with. The class work may be too hard or too easy. If this is the case, then you need to discuss the problem with your child's teacher. Together you can find some relief and make adjustments, so your child can feel successful again.

❇ Your child may not be able to see or hear well or may have a fear of asking questions in class or taking part in classroom discussions. Make sure any physical problems are taken care of.

❇ Your child may have an emotional problem, which can certainly get in the way of learning. In this case, you should start with your family doctor or visit with the school counselor or mental health department for advice. Don't let emotional problems get in the way of school success.

❇ Your child may have negative feelings toward classmates or teachers and feel that other people keep him from learning. In this case, it is your task to try to change the child's view of the cause of his failure. A gentle reminder to try harder would be in order. If your children know that you are not satisfied with the amount and quality of time and effort they put into school work, you might find some improvement. You may need to help your child set up a realistic schedule for studying and a quiet place without distractions.

✱ Using appropriate praise for small successes goes a long way toward improving motivation. Be careful about giving praise for simple tasks that require little effort. If you praise everything equally, your child will soon learn that your praise means nothing. The child may get the message that you feel they do not have much ability.

Unmotivated students frequently blame other factors, such as a poor teacher or "I'm not smart," or "Good students are lucky." While these factors may affect success in school, your child may be exaggerating the influence of these factors. Students often prefer to ignore their own responsibility for their success or failure.

Motivation comes from within the person. I wrote this book because I wanted to. I scheduled the necessary time and had the energy to get it done on time. I also get enough rest, have a sound diet, and keep myself physically fit, so that I feel good about myself. That's what motivation is really all about. Children must feel good about themselves to be motivated.

WHY SOME CHILDREN ARE NOT MOTIVATED

Students' lack of motivation has concerned parents and teachers for a long time. In this country, we are proud of all the material things we give our kids, hoping they will be satisfied. We want our kids to have more than we had. We give them VCRs, TV, and telephones in their rooms. We try to keep them up with the kids next door and give in to all the latest fads.

All this good life has its problems, according to Bruce A. Waldin, a practicing psychologist. He says, "Giving children too much may be giving too little." Parents frequently comment, "Those kids have everything. I don't understand why their grades are so poor." Another common statement is "Jane did it again. She just isn't responsible and doesn't seem to care about anything."

Bruce Baldwin has identified some parental behaviors that just might contribute to raising children who are unmotivated, demanding, unappreciative, and rude. To see if you fit the description, see how many questions you answer yes to:

1. Too many toys. Is your child's room overflowing with toys and gadgets?
2. Giving in to demands. Do you usually give in to your child's demands for more things after only a token resistance?
3. Doing their homework. Do you help your child excessively with homework and other projects?
4. Giving in to latest fads. Do you let your child get all the latest fad toys and clothes?
5. Unrestricted money to spend. Do you give your child unearned money to spend whenever he wants it?
6. Inconsistent discipline. Do you threaten to punish your child for breaking rules, then rarely follow through?
7. Overprotecting. Do you often protect your child from experiencing the consequences of inappropriate behavior and rule breaking?
8. Unlimited television. Do you permit your child to watch too much TV, even on school days, so he won't "bug" you?

DEVELOPING BETTER STUDY HABITS

As a parent, there are several things you can do to help your child improve his grades. Primarily, you must help your child develop better study habits and a better attitude about getting assignments completed. Your child needs the experience of "a job well done."

Developing good study habits, a set of tools helping to

increase the amount of information learned and prolonging the length of time information is remembered, takes some of your time and your child's time. Good study habits are not easy for some students, but they can be learned with your help. Since studying is thinking, it is important to make your home a place where it is easy for your child to think and to do homework. Your child can concentrate on only one thing at a time, and you can choose what your child thinks about.

Study areas should be free from noise and other distractions. You need to take charge of the student's environment. You need to turn off the TV and radio and music. Some students will tell you that they need to have loud music while studying. That is pure nonsense. Remember, they can do only one thing well at a time.

What is the best time for studying and doing homework? There are several very basic steps you can take to assure homework will be done and done on time. Your child needs your help in planning time efficiently.

Decide together on the best time to do homework, and then set that time according to your school's policy on homework. Five days out of the week is the usual. If there is no homework, that time can be used to review or read library books. Whatever plan you and your child decide on, stick to it. You may find an hour of concentrated study is better than two hours of distractions and interruptions.

Try planning on a study break. Depending on the age of your child, you might set a timer to be used as a signal for break time.

What is a good place to do homework? The answer might include the following:

✍ Good lighting.
✍ The right temperature. A room that is too cool is considered better than one that is too warm.

✍ A table or desk. Students should have enough space for writing and should be free of all distractions.

✍ Good posture. Sitting in a comfortable chair helps a student concentrate and stay alert. Discourage your child from lying down on a bed or on the floor. Lying down may be so relaxing that it will interfere with concentration.

✍ Adequate supplies and materials. Have the following items in a drawer or on a shelf, within easy reach: paper, pencil, pens, ruler, glue, eraser, paper clips, scissors, pencil sharpener, crayons, stapler, and dictionary.

Be a source of encouragement for your child's efforts. Be available for questions, but remember it is their homework, not yours.

During the planned study time eliminate distractions as follows:

✍ Be sure other family members are not moving around or talking.

✍ If there are young children, make sure they are out of earshot of the studying child.

✍ Keep work areas uncluttered.

✍ Telephone calls should not be allowed to interrupt. Let your child know there will be no telephone calls during study time.

✍ Friends are not to come by during study time.

✍ Students should not be expected to do chores for parents during study time.

These ideas have worked in homes where children are successful and happy students. Parents need to share the responsibility with their school in helping children become better students.

GETTING THE MOST OUT OF YOUR PERSONAL COMPUTER

More and more families own computers, and the numbers will increase as time goes by. Families are now tapped into electronic mail. They can send and receive messages through their home computers using a modem and phone line. Your computer equipment allows the family to browse the Internet, the global network of computers, linking you with universities, corporations, and governments. More than 35 million American homes have personal computers with modems. Many of these families are missing out on opportunities that can benefit their children's learning.

Like television, computers have their dangers. Children can get pornographic material very easily. The best way to safeguard your children is to take the time to learn computers, modems, the Internet software, and on-line services, so you can monitor your child's use. This way, you can also help your child use the computer as something more than a video game machine. There are excellent educational programs that can be purchased for children to practice skills introduced at school.

These ideas will help you and your children launch into the world of computers:

✍ The next time your child is assigned a report on the Civil War, he can tap into the Library of Congress for a wealth of information.

✍ Your children can e-mail a letter to the editor of a magazine to which they subscribe.

✍ Your child can send thank-you letters to friends and relatives in another city, state, or country.

✍ Your child can develop a pen pal friendship with a child or relative in another state or country.

✍ Use e-mail to keep in touch with an older brother or sister who goes away to college.

✍ Create a family newsletter, and let your child be the news reporter. He can interview grandparents and other relatives, compile the articles, and e-mail it to the whole family by the click of the "send" key.

✍ A student taking a foreign language can go on-line with a service in French, German, or Spanish. They can even practice with students from countries where that language is spoken.

✍ Many universities and colleges provide students with computers and free Internet access, so you can keep up with what is going on with your older student.

Establish e-mail ground rules. Insist that your child ask permission each time before logging on. Instruct your child not to give out any personal information, such as home address or telephone number. Since e-mail travels over phone lines and through many computers, the messages could be read by strangers.

Teach your children to use good manners when using e-mail. Answer messages promptly, politely, and briefly. Address e-mail letters properly, using a person's correct title, such as "Dear Librarian" or "Dear Editor." Use appropriate closings, such as "Sincerely, Nick" or "Your friend, Sara."

Encourage your child to use complete sentences and to end each sentence with a period.

These e-mail addresses will help get you started:

Library of Congress: icweb@loc.gov
National Geographic's World Magazine: ngsforum@aol.com

In addition, a magazine many people find helpful when browsing the World Wide Web is *Internet World*, available for $29/year at 20 Ketchum St., Westport, CT 06880.

As a new generation of computers becomes available, excellent used computers will be selling for under $500. Watch newspaper ads, and don't be afraid to ask knowledgeable people before making a purchase.

Section Two

START EARLY—Building Reading Skills

**Chapter 4: Getting Your Child
Hooked on Reading
Chapter 5: Encouraging Your Child
to Read**

> *You may have tangible wealth untold;*
> *Caskets of jewels and coffers of gold.*
> *Richer than I you can never be,*
> *I had a mother who read to me.*
>
> **—"The Reading Mother" by Strickland Gillian**
> **from *Best Loved Poems of the American People***

Chapter Four

GETTING YOUR CHILD
HOOKED ON READING

PROFILE OF A PERSON WHO READS

A person who reads books for pleasure and who reads newspapers and magazines for information has the following traits:

- ✍ Reads the newspapers and magazines about candidates running for public office, listens to debates, becomes informed on issues and votes in every election. A well-informed population is more apt to maintain a democratic form of government.
- ✍ Develops interpersonal skills, thus is more apt to be a stable marriage partner and will take responsibility for raising children and is less likely to divorce.
- ✍ Will have an income that is much greater than the average individual who does not read books, newspapers, and magazines. Is more apt to be retrained for a new career, if necessary, and to read information that will lead to a promotion.

66

✍ Is more willing to run for public office at the local, state, and federal level.

✍ Is less likely to have a police record, other than a traffic violation, than the nonreader. A person who does a lot of reading is four times less likely to get into trouble with the law or spend time in prison.

✍ Will have children who will also want to read for information and pleasure. They will excel in school and are more apt to be successful as students and to go to college and be successful.

✍ Are not as apt to experience mental illness. They tend to have a more optimistic attitude about the future and are more likely to solve personal problems.

✍ Is more apt to visit foreign countries and travel to new and interesting places. Is more likely to attend concerts, attend plays, visit museums, and appreciate the visual arts.

✍ Will be known as friendly, a good conversationalist, and a good leader. In general, will have a good time and will be the kind of person others will want to be around. Is more willing to listen to both sides of an issue.

✍ Is less apt to abuse alcohol and drugs, simply because people who read for information and pleasure feel good about themselves and enjoy what they are doing.

A parent of a preschooler asked me, "Why should I read to him?" My answer was that regular reading aloud to children strengthens reading, writing, expressive oral language, and rich vocabulary, and it develops their imagination. Reading aloud to your children stimulates their interest, their emotional development, their imagination, and their speaking vocabulary.

The primary learning method of young children is imitation. They imitate what they hear and what they see. This ability to imitate allows the 12-month-old child to say his first word. By age 2, the average child expands his vocabulary to include nearly 300 words. That figure is 900 words by the third year, 1600 by age four, and 20,000 by age five. The average adult uses less than 20,000 words. A child's language development is extremely rapid.

If your child hears the English language as spoken by some of the characters on TV, such as the Teenage Mutant Ninja Turtles or Beavis and his pal on MTV, then your child will model the speech of those TV characters. The danger with that language is that it is different from the English language a student is asked to read, write, and speak in public schools or college. The problem with "TV language" is that too much of it is improperly constructed. TV jargon is not what your child needs as a model.

Children who are raised on too much TV and who listen to rock music can be recognized by a speech pattern that is punctuated by "you know" and "I mean like...." These grunts and groans of rock music can hardly be the kind of model you want for your child's future success as a student.

Good children's literature offers a wealth of language for young children to use as a model. Good literature is colorful, rich in meaning, correct, and it offers your child the best hope of expressing feeling and assuring success as a student.

How old should a child be before you start reading to her? The parent's reading voice has the most calming effect on the very young infant. There is evidence that the mother can read to a child starting at six months in the pregnancy. The child in the womb is capable of distinguishing positive or negative tones in the mother's voice. The mother who starts reading while the child is still in the womb is conditioning her child for her first lesson in listening and learning.

Parents frequently ask, "Can a six-month-old child understand what is being read to her?" On the day of birth, read to your newborn. You are less interested in "understanding" than you are with "conditioning" your child to your soothing reading voice and to books.

Studies of early readers and of children who are good readers tell us that these children learned to read without difficulty and had the following factors present in the home environment.These four factors are found in *every* home of children who were early readers:

☞ The child was read to as a young child on a regular basis. Additionally, the parents were avid readers and led their children to books by example. Parents read aloud—books, package labels, street signs, billboards, and anything else that was available.

☞ A multitude of printed material—books, magazines, newspapers, comics—were all available in the home.

☞ Ample paper and pencils were available for the entire family. Without exception, the starting point of curiosity about the written language was an interest and encouragement in scribbling and drawing. The children soon developed an interest in copying and writing letters of the alphabet.

☞ Parents stimulated the child's interest in reading and writing by answering their questions and giving appropriate praise for their efforts in reading and writing. Parents took their children to the public library frequently, encouraged them to spend their money on books, and bought their children books as presents for birthdays and other events.

All you need to have a child who learns to read on her own and who learns to read easily when given reading instruction by the classroom teacher is to take the time to read to your child every day. Put her drawings on the refrigerator door or bulletin board. Take the time and patience to answer questions and ask your child questions. Point out signs along streets and highways.

Jim Trelease, in his book, *The Read Aloud Handbook*, states that "when you read aloud to children you are fulfilling one of the noblest duties of cultured man." It is this sharing and enriching that allows a culture to grow among people. Artists, writers, and musicians alone cannot keep a culture alive. They must be backed by the enthusiasm of a multitude of parents who treasure their heritage and will devote their energies to keeping its flames aglow.

The mother who sits through music and dance recitals and the father who puts down the evening paper to help his son or daughter with the drawing of a tree and the teacher who reads to the class every day are the real lifeblood of a culture. To them must fall the responsibility to pass it on.

READING TO YOUR CHILD STARTS EARLY

A mother read aloud Kipling stories to her baby while breastfeeding. She read aloud whatever she was interested in. By six months, the baby would listen to anything the mother read. That baby grew up hooked on reading and graduated from Purdue with honors. Reading is the most soothing thing a mother can do for a baby. Yes, children are born with an amazing capacity for listening.

A university study shows that if a child is read to once a day, she will become an average reader. If parents read to a child twice a day and talk to the child frequently, the child will become a superior reader. If not read to by parents, the child will struggle with reading and may never enjoy it.

The question is, how often and for how long should you read to your child? Read as often and as long as your child wants to be read to. Most toddlers will sit and listen to a story or look at a picture book for up to 15 minutes, then will want to do something else. It is best if you read two or three times daily.

Reading to your child develops these positive attributes:

1. Builds positive attitudes toward reading.
2. Exposes your child to a variety of literature.
3. Expands your child's greater knowledge.
4. Gives your young child a richer vocabulary.
5. Increases the bonds between parent and child that are essential for future development.

These principles will help you get started reading to your child and will keep you reading to your preschooler:

✄ Know your child's attention span, and don't go beyond it. If your child has trouble sitting still, read while she is playing. Be sure to make reading aloud a pleasant experience.
✄ Get to know your child's interests. Your child may be interested in fairy tales. Follow your child's lead in choosing books. You might say, "Pick out a book that you want me to read to you."
✄ Take time to talk to your child about the book before, during, and after reading, with emphasis on discussion. Try to avoid right or wrong answers. Be a good listener. If the story provokes discussion, let your child talk.
✄ Ask questions about the story when you read to your preschooler. Be positive by accepting all of your child's thoughts and then discuss other possible solutions. The reason for your asking questions is to get your preschooler to think about the story and to give your child a better understanding of the story and the author's message. Try asking, "What do you think this story will be about?"

71

"What do you think will happen next?" Did you like the way the story ended?" "How would like the story to end?"

✂ When your preschooler is ready and knows the story well enough, let him read with you. At first, you might want to pause, so your child can supply a word you are certain she knows. Later, encourage your child to repeat refrains with you from well-known stories, such as "The Gingerbread Man" or "The Three Little Pigs."

✂ To help your child get the most out of a book, read the book yourself first. Then you will know how to get your child excited about the story.

✂ Your child might enjoy getting involved with the story by acting it out or dressing up like one of the characters in the story. Ask your child to describe favorite parts or characters.

✂ Try to link the ideas in the book to events in your child's life. This will help make the story more personal and meaningful. For example, "Do you remember when we went camping? How was our trip different from the trip in the story?"

✂ Try varying what you read—fiction, animal stories, humor, fairy tales, legends, adventure, history, and suspense.

Reading to your preschooler is the most important activity you can do to get him ready for learning. Most children who are read to two or three times daily from birth on are able to learn to read on their own before going to school. There are lots of success stories about three-year-old children knowing how to read.

With the abundance of picture books that are illustrated in full color, it is hard for any child not to be interested in wanting to read. Your public library has excellent selections. Also, you can purchase picture books at garage sales and used book stores.

THE IMPORTANCE OF PARENTS' ATTITUDES TO-WARD READING

What parents do about reading speaks louder than what parents say!!

Ask yourself these questions:

✂ How many times have you read aloud to your children this week?

✂ How many times have they seen you reading books this month?

✂ Are books available and encouraged in your home?

✂ How often do you read together as a family?

✂ Do you have a regular storytime established in your routine?

Whether your child blossoms into an enthusiastic, skilled reader has much to do with the reading climate in your home. You have a powerful influence on the reading interest, skills, and more importantly, the love of reading developed by your children.

Consider the following techniques which should be used when sharing books in your home:

✦ Select books that are appropriate to the interest levels and ages of your children. Your public librarian will be glad to help you.

✦ First read the books to get an idea of the content and the story line.

✦ Try to read with expression.

✦ Sit with your child so that you both can see the pictures and the words. If you have several children, let them take turns sitting by you. Laps are just right for young children.

✦ Keep the children as close to you as possible.

✦ Let your younger children turn the pages if they want to.
✦ Take turns reading. You read for awhile, then let your child
read. Be helpful and interested.
✦ Ask questions as you go along, but try not to interrupt the
flow of the story too often.
✦ Think about your child's attention span. A very young child
is not going to sit still for as long as an older child.
✦ Occasionally, tell the story instead of reading it.

When children see reading as a major activity in the lives of the adults—mothers and fathers—around them, they soon realize that reading is important. When you take the time each day to read together as a family, you are not only providing that much-needed time in which to practice reading, but you are also showing your children that you consider reading important enough to take the time to do it.

The problem is that some kids start school primed for learning to read, while to others it is a mystery. Those kids struggle and rarely ever catch up with the kids who are read to. Children who are read to by their parents from birth on are frequently on the honor role at school. Why would this be so?

There are several answers to that question:

1) Good books excite children about reading.
2) They develop important language skills.
3) Reading improves social development.
4) Reading develops problem-solving skills.
5) Children score much higher on reading and math tests.
6) Children develop good listening skills.
7) Reading develops a close bond between parent and child.
8) Reading develops expressive oral language, which leads to
better readers and better writers.
9) Children tend to be well-behaved because they are getting
positive parental attention.

It has been estimated that the typical middle-income child has already spent nearly 2,000 hours of one-to-one reading, cuddled up with dad or mom, having fun talking and reading, which develops a very positive attitude toward reading and books by the time they start first grade.

Some parents neglect to promote reading by reading to their children at home. So their children start the first day of school not yet ready for learning to read. They may not even be ready to listen to a story read to the class by the teacher.

Here are seven pointers on how to make reading aloud enjoyable to both you and your child:

1. For beginners, choose a picture book that has few words, such as *The Very Busy Spider* by Eric Carle. For those learning to read, try *Ramona the Pest* by Beverly Cleary. For third and fourth graders, start with *Charlotte's Web* by E.B. White. For fifth and sixth graders, read *My Side of the Mountain* by Jean George. The public library has lots of good books, and the librarian is always happy to help you.
2. Encourage your child to think by asking "what" questions, such as "What do you think will happen next?" or "What is that?"
3. Use appropriate praise, such as "That's right," or "I'm proud of you for knowing the answer."
4. Listen to your child so you will know her interests. Discuss whatever your child brings up. This will develop expressive oral language.
5. Learn to ask open-ended questions, such as, "What do you see on this page?" or "What do you think will be on the next page?"
6. Expand your child's language skills. For example, if they say, "The fish swims," you should reply by saying, "Yes, the fish is swimming in the water."
7. If you are just starting out on the adventure of reading to

your children, choose books you will enjoy reading. If you like the story, then your children will like it.

READING AT HOME IS IMPORTANT

With busy schedules, many parents express concern that their children don't read. Well, there is something you can do with a little planning. You can turn off the TV and radio and gather your little flock together and say, "We are going to read at home." After all, the school has them for six hours a day, and you have them the rest of the time. The home should be a place to practice the skills taught by your child's teacher.

✦ Get your family together and agree on a time when everyone in the family will read. Yes, read anything— magazines, newspaper, books, and picture books for the preschoolers. Your public library will help you.

✦ Agree on a place—living room or den. You must all be in the same area.

✦ Before you start, have family members select any reading material.

✦ Start out with an agreed-upon time, such as 15 minutes, then extend it to 30 minutes daily. Yes, every day at the same time. Then it becomes tradition and habit.

✦ Each person reads silently until the time is up. Even your preschoolers can "read" picture books or look at pictures in magazines, like *National Geographic*.

✦ The rules for reading should be agreed on before starting the session.

1. All members of the family who are present must sit quietly with reading materials.

2. There can be no talking or interrupting another person's reading.

3. No one needs to be questioned about what has been read.

The emphasis will be on reading for pleasure.

4. Parents and adults present must read as a good model for the kids.

5. Put a sign on the door, "PLEASE DON'T DISTURB — FAMILY IS READING."

6. Tell everyone to announce to their friends not to call by phone during this reading session.

7. If the phone does ring or someone comes to the door, simply say, "Sorry, our family is reading and can't be disturbed. We will call you back."

✦ When the time is up, the family can go back to other activities. Family members may want to discuss or share what they have read, but there should be no pressure to do this.

GOOD BOOKS TO HELP CHILDREN THROUGH TOUGH TIMES

A parent of an eight-year-old once said to me, "My son is having a tough time accepting his grandfather's recent death. What can I do?" My suggestion was to get the book, *My Grandpa Died Today* by Joan Fassier and read it to the child, while other members of the family listen in.

Every child deals with a lot of feelings and situations about which they have questions. By reading and discussing stories with your child, you can provide a means of exploring emotions and a method for dealing with those emotions.

Good books can help children of all ages recognize their feelings and make parents aware of what children do and don't do to cope with these feelings. A child is more apt to accept himself if, through stories, he sees other children with similar problems, worries, or conflicts. The great value in books is that discussing a character in a story is a safe and impersonal way of looking at a problem; it is nonaccusing, nonlecturing, and nonjudgmental, because the child is not personally involved.

By reading a book to your child, your role becomes that of thought provoker. You will want to discuss in a comfortable manner what the character in the book was feeling, what motivated the character's actions, what the character might have done differently, and what effect the character's choices might have in the long run.

One of your main tasks as a parent is to help a child recognize her emotions and find acceptable outlets for those emotions. You should consider reading to your child on a regular basis, especially at bedtime. Reading books to children provides an opportunity to discuss different topics, feelings, and ideas. Reading books with a child can remind us of what a child's world is like. Children's books can put us in touch with what is and what isn't important to a child.

The following list of books about dealing with specific problems are just right for children preschool through age eight. They can be found in the library and in bookstores.

My Grandpa Died Today by Joan Fassier.
The Dead Bird by Margaret Wise Brown.
The Tenth Good Thing About Barney by Judith Viorst.

An excellent source of books to meet the problems that face growing up is *The Book Finder: When Kids Need Books* by Sharon Dryer, published by American Guidance Service.

Chapter Five

ENCOURAGING YOUR CHILD TO READ

"Few children learn to love books by themselves. Someone has to lure them into the wonderful world of the written word; someone has to show them the way."
—Orville Prescott, *A Father Reads to His Children*

FATHERS INFLUENCE FAMILY READING

Fathers or father images are important role models for children becoming readers. Children of all ages need the approval and influence of a father. A father has been defined as "someone to look up to no matter how tall you are."

How can you influence your children to read more and to practice reading skills taught during the school year? Very simple. These functional reading ideas will prove useful:

☆ You can be seen reading the newspaper or magazine and, yes, a book. "Monkey see, monkey do."
☆ Let your child help you in reading directions to put a bike together or the directions to build something.
☆ Read the how-to books on a subject like plumbing, carpentry, or gardening.

☆ Read a manual to fix the family car (then take it to a real mechanic to have it fixed after you goof it up).

☆ When you are on a trip, let your child collect brochures and read the maps.

☆ Take your child to the library. You check out a book, and have your child check out books to read, or for you read aloud to your child.

☆ Read to your children daily. They'll love you for it.

☆ Try setting aside a time when the TV is turned off and the whole family reads. No talking or playing games—just reading. Even nonreaders can look at pictures or pretend to be reading.

Fathers have a positive influence on reading. Studies show that more than 70 percent of remedial reading students are boys. In the past, we have rationalized that boys develop later. In many European countries, the trend is reversed—girls outnumber boys in remedial reading classes.

So what is the difference? The difference is our cultural values. American boys are in remedial classes because their fathers have convinced them that the most important things in life are the things the boys see their dads get excited about—little league baseball, football, basketball.

In elementary school, nearly 90 percent of the teachers are women and, if a boy seldom sees an adult male reading in the school or at home, boys are apt to think that reading is not for males. American culture has given boys a bad rap when it comes to reading. Fathers can play catch or shoot baskets in the backyard and still be intellectually involved with their sons. Fathers can play ball after dinner and on the same night read to their children for 15 minutes. Fathers can take their sons to a game on Friday and then to the public library on Saturday to check out some books to read.

Children who see their adult role model enjoying

reading, taking their children to the library for story hour and checking out library books, giving books for special occasions, reading the newspaper and sharing part of what he reads do become lifetime readers and lifetime achievers.

School records indicate that boys' scores decline when their fathers are absent from the home. A school in California reported that boys in fourth, fifth, and sixth grades: 1) scored much higher in reading if they were read to by their fathers and 2) read more and scored higher when their fathers read for pleasure, when compared with boys whose fathers did little or no recreational reading.

PRESCHOOL

To point out the importance of parents' role in the education of their children, the Carnegie Commission on Ready to Learn reported in 1991 that over one-third of the kindergarteners were not ready for the first grade. The kindergarten teacher had the children for roughly 200 hours. From birth to the sixth years, the parents had them for 52,000 hours. Contemporary parents need to begin to take a more active and responsible role in getting children ready for learning.

In preparing children for reading and learning, in general, one-third of parents do an excellent job of preparing their children for learning, and theirs are the children on the honor rolls and getting the top grades. While one-third do an average or good job and have kids getting B's and C's, it is the bottom one-third, whose getting D's and F's, which cause the teachers to work so hard to try to get them to read and achieve.

These are the kids who find themselves in remedial classes across the country. They are the ones who are behavior problems and dropouts. In many cases, they are the ones getting in trouble, appearing in our courts and filling up our prisons.

It is this one-third on the lower end of achievement who present a challenge to American classroom teachers. As one teacher said, "The best students don't wait for the bottom one-third to catch up." Many of the bottom one-third tend to want to drop out and give up. For those children whose parents cannot or will not do their job, the teachers become the last hope before adulthood. Since classroom teachers do work hard to find ways to turn the reluctant reader into a child who enjoys reading, that child has a much greater chance of growing up and doing the right things to be a contributing member of society. Remember, the teacher needs a supporting set of parents, especially a reading father.

HOW TO HELP A RELUCTANT READER

A reluctant reader is a child who does not like to read. He or she may lack reading skills such as vocabulary or word-analysis skills. For these children, learning to read is hard. Of course, if a task is hard, then the child soon gives up and dislikes it. If you have a child who is a reluctant reader, then these ideas will help your child discover the joy of reading.

All parents want their children to be able to absorb information from reading. Most reluctant readers would rather watch TV or play video games. Too often, hurried teachers don't have the time to help reluctant readers. You, the parent, can help your children understand the importance of reading by your own behavior and attitudes.

There's one thing you can't do with reluctant readers: motivate them by arguing about the importance of reading.

The following four items will lead your reluctant reader to the joy of reading:

1. Interest. Find out what your child is interested in. If your reluctant reader likes sports, then get sports magazines.

School librarians tell us that boys will go to sports magazines like ducks to water. Why not find hunting stories for a reluctant reader who likes to hunt? Some little girls like horses. There are lots of good stories about horses. Some are classics. Ask your public librarian about magazine subscriptions about horses.

2. Reading level. Make sure that the reading material is at a reading level your child can understand. Good readers develop vocabulary by stretching themselves. They find challenging reading material. When reluctant readers are forced to read material that contains difficult vocabulary, you are only reinforcing their sense of inadequacy.

3. Introduce stories. Once you've found your child's interest and easy-to-read books, read the first few pages or chapter aloud. Now you are sharing the greatest gift you can give—your time. You are the child's role model in developing the reading habit, and you are there to ask questions or initiate dialogue about the action or characters in the story.

4. Read aloud. Reading stories aloud on a regular basis is the best way to develop a love of reading. Choose books that start quickly. Humor or mystery will always be popular. Give your reluctant reader a taste of the story and leave him hanging. When reading aloud, stop and ask questions about the action or characters. Just before the end of a segment, ask for predictions about the outcome. Your goal is to get your reluctant reader involved in the story.

Few children can resist a good story. Hook your reluctant reader with a particular book, and the power of the good story becomes an immediate incentive and reward to continue.

Frequently, all it takes is for a reluctant reader to get through one good book he's enjoyed. It will give him the confidence to tackle another and then another. Reading is like anything else. With practice, reading can improve. As his reading improves, so will his confidence in himself. You will have helped create a positive cycle and given him one of the most important gifts a child can possess—the joy of reading.

The following tips will help you find a book your child can read:

☞ Read the cover to see if it is the kind of book your reluctant reader would like. If it doesn't meet your child's interest, pass it up.

☞ Read the first part. If the first ten pages are not exciting enough to hold your interest, set it aside. It is the author's job to make the reader want to read the story.

☞ Five-finger test. Go to the middle of the book and put up a finger for every word you think your child will not know. By the end of the page, if you have put up five fingers, put the book aside. It will be too difficult.

☞ Once you've found an author whom your reluctant reader likes, stay with that author. Many times authors have series with the same characters. Reluctant readers are apt to pick up another book if they know they can handle the vocabulary.

LANGUAGE EXPERIENCE HELPS POOR READERS

A thoughtful, but frustrated mother wanted to hire a tutor to teach her nine-year-old child to read. The child's reading level was pre-primer (first grade). However, the child could understand a story read to her at the fourth-grade reading level.

After working with the child a few minutes, we discovered the child had well-developed expressive oral language skills. I used the old time-tested Language Experience

Approach to reading, and it worked. The mother was elated and so was the child.

The secret to this child's success in reading came after the child told a neat story about skiing on Saturday: "Sunday, I went skiing. I learned how to go up the ski tow by myself. A couple of times I fell off. Then, once the tow hit me in the face and made me go in the snow. It did not hurt. I went up the tow with Pat, a friend of my mom's, and I went up to the top of the ski hill."

We used her story to identify words:

- I asked the child how many times "snow" appeared in the story. Then, by drawing a line around each word, "snow," they were found promptly.
- I asked how many times she could find the word "up" in the story. All were underlined quickly and enthusiastically.
- I read the story twice to the child while she watched.
- Then, we read the story orally together, using periods, commas, etc., for good expression.
- Then the child read the story alone and knew such big words as "learned," "couple," "friend," and "myself."
- We looked for words with long vowel sounds, with silent "e," such as "made." Then, together we made up our own list, as in "made," "face," "cake," and "case." We discussed how these words were alike.
- From her story, we made up a spelling list, such as "go," "up," "of," "me," etc.

Why does the Language Experience Approach to Reading work like magic on kids who are having problems with reading?

1. The child is able to freely talk about an experience, while the parent writes exactly what the child says.

2. While you are writing, pronounce each word aloud while the child is watching.
3. The words and sentences are in the child's own language.
4. It is easy for a child to read his own story because it is in his language.

The whole point is that what a child can talk about, an adult can write. The child can easily read his own story, because he knows what it says. Parents of children in first and second grades can easily do this and not interfere with any reading program that is being used in the child's classroom.

There is one caution. Don't change the language the child uses. Write down exactly what the child says.

This procedure helps the child understand that 1) writing is talking on paper; 2) reading is simply reading what someone else said on paper; and 3) because the child naturally talks in sentences, he can see that oral language is also written in sentences. Use lots of appropriate praise for telling a good story and encourage your child to practice reading the story and then read it to another member of the family.

By the way, refrigerator doors were made for taping kids' stories on.

EXPRESSIVE ORAL LANGUAGE NECESSARY FOR READING

Why spend time teaching expressive oral language? The answer is very simple, but too often overlooked by all of us. We all want our children to learn to read. We spend a great deal of time and energy trying to teach them to read, and if they don't come up to our expectations, we get frustrated. The children also get frustrated and will probably give up, because they lack the expressive oral language and vocabulary necessary to make the progress in reading that we would like them to make. Past studies clearly tell us that to be good readers and to be able to write well, children must bring to school a wealth of good language, based on firsthand experiences.

We do know that children who come to school with a large vocabulary and who are able to express themselves easily make the greater achievement in reading and writing. Reading is "being able to read what is written on paper," and writing is "talking on paper." So you see, expressive oral language is essential to reading and writing.

We do know that if children have limited expressive oral language, then they will have limited reading and writing achievement. Most studies in the field of reading tell us that giving children the opportunity to talk cannot be overdone. Children need a wealth of experiences in order to have something to talk about.

Parents can start doing several things to increase their children's expressive oral language. Try some of these:

❖ Encourage your child to talk about experiences and activities without making judgmental statements.
❖ Take time to read to your child daily. Improving listening skills improves vocabulary and gives children a model for language.
❖ When appropriate, take your children with you, so they can have rich experiences on which to base their vocabulary and will have something to talk about.
❖ Use mealtime as an opportunity for family conversation. Let the children talk and express themselves without your making judgments. You might even consider friendly arguments.
❖ Take time every day to listen to each child. Be patient.
❖ Read to your child daily and discuss the content with your child. Ask questions about the story and accept reasonable answers.

I'm sure you can find other ways to improve your child's expressive oral language. If you are concerned and need help, you can contact your child's classroom teacher to get ideas. When the home and the school work together, then real progress can take place. You can't expect the school to do it all.

HOW TO ENCOURAGE CHILDREN TO READ

The key to children's learning to read is the positive environment the home has toward reading and language development. Some of these ideas will work on older children with some adaptation.

★ Read to your child daily and talk with him frequently. This will increase the child's vocabulary and language skills.
★ Encourage your child to tell "pretend stories" about pictures in a storybook.
★ Play games with directions words, such as "Put the book into (or below or behind) the bag."
★ Encourage the playing of simple action games, such as "Walk to the door slowly." "Open the door carefully." Use words like quietly, quickly, slowly, and carefully."
★ Play describing (adjective) games. For instance, you might ask your child to find something in a room that is *big, little, soft, hard, furry*, and so on.
★ Encourage your young child to draw pictures and then tell stories about the drawings. You will want to write the story, so that it can be read again to the child. Small books can be made of the stories and drawings.
★ Avoid talking down to a young child. Children love new words and are quite good at vocabulary building. You'll be amazed at how many new words young children will use if they hear them used.

★ Discover with your child the wonders of this world. Let them talk about what they see and feel. Try not to respond with "Yes, I know that." You should respond with "That's very interesting," or "I'm glad you know that."

★ Always try not to react with extreme glee or disappointment when your child relates occurrences or make-believe stories. Fantasy and imagination should be encouraged, as long as the child recognizes the differences between fantasy and reality.

★ Take your child to the library. The child should be proud to own and use a library card. Your librarian can help you and your child select books.

★ Take the necessary time to spend a few minutes with your child on a daily basis. Every child has a right to individual attention from the parent. Children have a need for the parent to spend quality time with them. Children frequently misbehave when they don't get enough attention from their parents. Some children will misbehave if it means attaining even negative attention from them.

★ Sharpen your listening skills. You need to begin to listen to your children, so they can practice expressive oral language and you will know what your children are thinking about and what is troubling them. When your children get older, they will be in the habit of coming to you with personal problems. Be sure you avoid lecturing or being openly critical.

If you feel you don't have time for these kinds of activities, then you should begin to reevaluate how you are spending your time. Your child's early years are very critical in their intellectual development and emotional stability.

If you start doing these kinds of activities, you'll soon begin to see your child become happier, more secure, better behaved, and you might even like your child and begin to appreciate him more. If your child is in school, he will soon begin to learn more, behave better, and like school.

KNOW THE VALUE OF READING POETRY

Here are seven good reasons why parents should read poetry to their children, starting at birth and continuing through the upper elementary grades:

1. Nursery rhymes are babies' and young children's first exposure to poetry. As they sit in your lap and listen to the repetition of sounds, an entire new dimension of language opens up before them.
2. Many adults equate poetry with memorization of lines, which is unfortunate. For young children, poetry is a delightful language set to music. The sing-song quality of rhythm and rhymes fascinates children and motivates them to repeat in their minds what they have just heard with their ears.
3. The rhyming aspect of poetry is actually a reading readiness tool. A young child who cannot yet read can often supply the ending to a verse. One reason children love to hear Dr. Suess books is that his stories almost always rhyme.
4. Poetry should be a regular component of your children's reading experiences. Poetry runs the gamut of human emotions and permits children to share the feelings and visions of the poet. Poetry teaches children comedy and tragedy and has the ability to transport them to Medieval England on one page and into the 21st century on the very next page.
5. Poetry encourages children to explore language and play with words. It helps children to discover patterns, both in, through, and on paper.
6. As children grow, their experiences with poetry should

progress from nursery rhymes to books of poems. You may wish to read to your child some books that contain a single poem and books that contain collections of poems. Either way, take time to read poetry aloud to your children, so they can savor the rhythmic flow of your voice and the melody of the words.

7. Poetry can be a playful entertainer on a rainy afternoon, or a special guest that shares holiday festivities, or a bedtime companion who lulls a child off to sleep.

Here are some suggestions for putting poetry into your children's lives:

★ Periodically copy a funny poem onto a napkin or paper and tuck the poem into your child's lunch bag or notebook. The surprise addition to the lunch or notebook will most likely be shared with friends.

★ As part of family birthdays or other special occasions, help your children compose limericks about family members, then use the limerick as part of the gift wrap for the person's present. Limericks are very popular with children and contain the following format: a five-line poem in which the first, second, and last lines rhyme. The third and fourth lines are usually short, and most rhyme only with each other. Example:

> There was a young man from Trevizes
> Whose ears were of different sizes,
> The left one was small,
> And of no use at all;
> With the right one he won several prizes.

★ Because children seem to prefer contemporary poetry, encourage them to create their own poetry describing a personal experience. Show them examples of free-verse poetry, in which there is a lack of rhyme and predictable meter. (The public librarian can help you find good books to get you started.)

★ Help your children to make an unusual type of autograph book. On each page of the book, spell out one of their friend's names vertically.

S aturday I go fishing!

T uesday I go skiing.

A pril brings more fishing.

N ovember watch the clouds go by.

Then the friend must describe himself, using the letters of his name as his special autograph.

A good book for preschoolers and first graders is *The Real Mother Goose*, illustrated by Blanch Wright. Your librarian can help you with good books for older children.

THE SOOTHING POWER OF WORDS

Bibliotherapy has been used to solve personal problems and promote coping behavior for nearly 150 years. The written word has had influence on human behavior ever since someone wrote the first word. Bibliotherapy, the use of reading materials to help solve emotional problems and to promote good mental health, was used by the military during World Wars I and II and with people in rehabilitation centers. Schools have used books and stories in helping children with problems for over 100 years.

Your teenager or younger child who is experiencing difficulties can read about other children who have had and solved the same problem. For example, your teenager who is having a hard time dealing with your divorce may find comfort after reading *Split Decision: Facing Divorce*. There's a children's book for every problem that a child must face. The book nearly always helps the child face or solve the problem.

There is tremendous comfort in knowing that someone else has gone through the same or a similar problem.

There are three steps in the process of bibliotherapy:

1) From their reading, children can see that they are not the only person with a particular problem;
2) Children will identify with fictional characters' lives through situations and will share common feelings with the characters;
3) Through reading, children can become more aware of human motivations and gain a better understanding of their own behavior.

The following books are only four of 725 books listed and reviewed in *The Bookfinder: When Kids Need Books* by Sharon Dreyer. You'll be able to find books that cover subjects like absent parents, bullies, cooperation, death, fear, jealously, and prejudice.

* Dealing with death. *Term Paper* by Ann Rinadli is the story of Nicki, who writes a term paper about her father's death. The book deals with the death of the father, sibling relationships, alcoholism, adult family relationships, guilt, feelings of love, and the meaning of rebellion.
* Dealing with anger. *The Ape Inside of Me* by Kim Platt is a story of a teenage boy who gives his uncontrollable temper a separate identity but realizes he'll never get anywhere until he takes control of "Kong." The book deals with anger, aggression, peer relationships, and self-discipline.
* Boy-girl relationships. *The Handsome Man* by Elisa Guest will appeal to many teenage girls and the conflicts that Alex feels toward her parents, the "handsome man" and her best friend. This warm and humorous novel deals with

the meaning of love, boy-girl relationships, family relationships, friendships, and the meaning of separation.

If you have a teenager who is a reluctant reader, a book addressing some personal problem may be just the thing to pique his interest.

Section Three

START EARLY—Building Social Skills
& Values
Chapter 6: Kids Need Social Skills
Chapter 7: Values Start at Home

When parents have little time for children,
a great vacuum will develop and
some kind of ideology will move in.

—Billy Graham

Chapter Six

KIDS NEED SOCIAL SKILLS

For a child to be a successful learner she needs to be able to get along with classmates. In other words, the child needs to develop "social acceptance."

To be socially acceptable, children must be taught self-control, cooperation, and good manners. The parent and teacher should cooperate in teaching important personal habits and acceptable social behavior. If a child is to be successful at school, she must have self-acceptance. You, the parent, might ask yourself these questions:

✓ Does my child like herself?
✓ Does my child have family acceptance, or does she follow family rules and accept responsibility in the home?
✓ Does my child have school and community acceptance?
✓ Does she follow school or community rules?

If your answer is no to one or more of the above questions, then you and the school must work together in helping the child develop self-acceptance. Many students fail because they lack the social skills to adjust to different situations. Many adults are unable to keep good jobs for the same reasons. It has been said that to be successful in school and work, 15 percent is skill and knowledge, and 85 percent is ability to get along with fellow students or workers.

BEING A GOOD FRIEND IS IMPORTANT

✦ Talk to your child on how people accept others. Have a friendly discussion on the most important qualities of a friend, such as honest, interesting, loyal, good sense of humor, etc.

✦ Talk with your child about making new friends, accepting others, wearing a smile, being loyal, being honest, being kind, etc.

✦ Ask your child what she thinks are the most important qualities of a friend. Now, list them in order of importance (avoid an argument with your child).

✦ On a piece of paper, have your child write the name of her very best friend. Underneath that name, have your child write three or four words that end in "y" that best describes the best friend. Example: friendly, loyalty.

✦ On another piece of paper, have your child write three or four words that she thinks best describe herself.

✦ Both of you write on a piece of paper what you think a good friend should be like. At this point, it is important for you to write a description of your best friend and then share it with your child.

CHILDREN NEED GOOD FRIENDSHIPS

What can I do about my child's friends?

Often parents and their children have disagreements about friends. We want our children to have friends that we approve of, but they may have a friend that we do not approve of, such as a bully or braggart. It is best to study your child's preference and attractions before attempting to interfere with her choices.

Next to parents, friends have more influence on your child than anyone else. As parents, you should be concerned about your child's relationships with other children. Experience tells us it takes only one bad friend to bring your child down, which may lead to trouble. So, helping your child at an early age to choose friends wisely is good advice.

What can parents do about friends who are not a good influence? First, know your own child's personality and needs. Friends should have a beneficial and corrective influence upon each other. Children need opportunities to associate with different personalities. For example, a withdrawn child may need the company of an outgoing friend; an overprotected child may need a more independent friend; a fearful child may benefit being in the company of a more courageous child; an immature child can benefit from the friendship of a mature friend. A child who is aggressive can be influenced by a child who is strong, but not belligerent. Your goal is to encourage corrective relationships by encouraging your child to have friends with personalities different from her own.

As parents, you need to be in charge from the very beginning. Some associations need to be discouraged. For example, children who may glamorize criminal behavior must be discouraged. They may attain "hero" status in school or in your neighborhood and serve as undesirable models for behavior. It takes a delicate system of checks and balances for your child to develop the full responsibility of choosing her friends and insuring that her choices are beneficial to personality development. If your child has trouble making friends and seems to spend most of her time alone, then you might try some of the following ideas that have worked for other parents:

* Provide opportunities for other children to be included in

family outings.
* Encourage your child to invite a friend to your home and spend the night, if appropriate.
* Have discussions about the importance of friendships by talking about your friends and why we all need friends.
* Set a good example for your child by having your own friends that you enjoy and consider important in your life.

We, as parents must encourage friendships. Your librarian can help you find good books on the importance of friendships. There are many books that young people can read that can be helpful.

Also, if you have some concerns, talk to your child's teacher and find out how you can work together. Don't be afraid to get professional help. Good friends are important!

BEING THE PEACEMAKER

Peacemaker: One who makes peace by reconciling parties at variance. A state of harmony among people or groups; the freedom from disorder normally present in a community.

When teaching your children to manage their own anger, be sure you don't use anger to get what you want. When children or adults resolve conflicts with aggression and violence, they are more likely to use some aggressive action to resolve the conflict. When you use corporal punishment, like hitting or spanking, you are teaching your children to use violence to solve their problems.

When families hold meetings to discuss problems, children learn how to resolve conflicts within a meeting context. Pick a time weekly when the entire family is present. Family members should be encouraged to bring problems to the meeting. Encourage family members bringing a problem to also bring a suggested solution.

To teach children how to solve differences, the parent should ask questions, "How did this problem come about?" "When did the problem start?" By asking questions, you are helping the children resolve the conflict. They need practice in problem-solving. If you solve it yourself, then your children will never gain experience.

Being a peace-maker means:

∗ Carefully trying to understand the needs and wants of another person.
∗ Working toward a solution in which both parties are satisfied.
∗ Using empathy when listening to others can avoid conflict and anger.
∗ At times, being assertive about your rights and position will help to avoid getting angry.
∗ Realizing that a win-win result is preferred to winning at all costs. Resolution in group situations is a true sign of success in peacemaking.

Examples:

∗ "I'm sorry I made you mad. I will try to be more thoughtful the next time."
∗ "Miss Jones, we were about to fight over who would be first, but we flipped a coin."
∗ "I think being the peacemaker is neat. When I'm about to get in a fight, I just walk away. I don't think it is worth it."
∗ "Our parents have told us kids over and over that fighting is not worth it, because someone always gets hurt. When resolving conflict with my brother and sister, we just sit down and talk about the conflict, and it works."

TEACHING YOUR KIDS TO SOLVE DIFFERENCES

Arguments and differences of opinion are normal between husband, wife, and children. Since husbands and wives are different, but equal, they tend to react to a conflict differently. Because they came from two different families, they have different wants, needs, values, and beliefs. Although these differences do exist, they do not need to create division within the home if conflicts are handled appropriately.

The inability of a husband and wife to handle conflict is a major source of divorce. Some may respond to an argument by withdrawing, pretending it did not happen, or becoming angry or defensive. Good healthy arguments involve expressing negative emotions in a constructive way. In most families, women were taught to believe that showing anger is not lady-like. So, they are conditioned to cry when frustrated, scared, or hurt.

Men, on the other hand, have learned to repress all their feelings, except anger. Men are more apt to "clam up," walk away, or react in a violent way when angry. They tend to want to fight.

Neither of these approaches will resolve differences to everyone's satisfaction. By parents resolving conflicts and making appropriate decisions, children in the family can imitate their approach.

These tips have worked for husbands and wives, so the children can also learn how to resolve conflict:

★ Make sure both of you have all the facts. Identify the problem. For example, the husband spent $150 on a car radio without talking it over with the wife.
★ Once you have identified the problem, clarify it by stating what should have happened. The wife could say, "We

agreed not to spend any more money this month. We were saving for a family trip." The husband might respond, "It was such a good buy, I couldn't resist."

★ After the two of you have cooled off, sit down and talk about family finances. Perhaps you need to budget so that bargains can be purchased. Most conflicts are from not understanding each other's needs. List ways to avoid problems over spending money. Be creative. Learn to accept that the two of you are different, but equal. Men's and women's differences are what make healthy marriages.

★ When you make a list of things to do to keep the problem from happening again, list all possible solutions, no matter how strange they may seem to you. Cross out the bad ideas later and leave the good ideas.

★ Because each of you has different values, ask how each alternative makes each of you feel about yourself and about each other. Do you still feel angry? If so, talk about other alternatives.

★ If the two of you can identify the best way to resolve differences to each person's satisfaction, then with practice you can solve other problems that are going to come up.

★ At a later date, evaluate your decisions. Are both of you happier with your solutions? Keep talking about how to resolve money problems that do come up.

★ When your children hear and see their parents resolve differences and come up with a logical solution, then the children can learn by example how to solve their little differences.

★ The key to any healthy family is the freedom to express feelings honestly and to listen to the other person without interrupting. Listening to the other person will provide understanding about how the other person feels.

If you are having trouble solving differences, contact a clergy who has experience and training in family counseling.

TEACHING GOOD MANNERS

Teaching good manners is one of the harder jobs of being a parent. In the days when families ate together every day, good manners were taught and reinforced. Many busy families sit down together to eat dinner only on special occasions, so parents don't want to spoil their meal by picking on their children's manners.

Our government must teach good etiquette to our U.S. diplomats. Parents are taking their children to etiquette school on Saturday afternoons. The parents seem to think saying "please" is a good idea.

Using humor to teach good etiquette is the best approach; for example, "You don't need to stab the chicken. It's already dead."

Make your instructions to your child as specific as possible. Kids are often unaware of how they appear or what they are doing wrong. Parents need to show or tell them exactly the behavior they want them to imitate.

Avoid unclear or vague statements such as " That's rude" and "Clean up," which give little information that children can act upon. Use statements such as, "People feel better when you look right in their eyes when you talk to them." Be sure to give specific instructions that children can follow and give the reason that such behavior makes sense.

At the dinner table, let the rules do the dirty work. Try to state the rule in neutral terms without criticizing. Saying, "Elbows do not go on the table," is better that giving a direct command, such as "Get your elbows off the table."

Once you've repeated the rule a few times, show your child that you expect him to take responsibility for minding his manners. Prompt your child by saying, "You know the right things to do or say. I must be having trouble hearing today, because I didn't hear you say a certain word."

It is helpful to get the idea across without saying a word. Next time you deliver a cup of orange juice to an ungrateful child, hold the drink just out of reach with a wink, a smile, or a cock of your head, until the appropriate response is used.

Whenever possible, to make a difficult task such as writing thank-you notes more enjoyable to your child, set out a treat, paper, and crayons for younger children. You can be the secretary and write down what your child dictates to an aunt and uncle. A preschooler can draw pictures to show grandpa how much he is enjoying his bow.

You can let your child use a camera. He can show grandpa the bow in action. Older children can use a computer to convey their appreciation.

Do the right things yourself. If you mind your manners by saying "please" and "thank you" when you ask your child to answer the phone or "excuse me" when you interrupt or bump into someone, your child will begin to understand how much better people feel when they are treated with respect and politeness. Ninety percent of teaching good manners is modeling. You can't expect your child to have good manners if you don't. Rudeness toward children is still rudeness.

A child will soon discover that, once he knows a few basic rules of etiquette, he will have the self-assurance to handle most situations with confidence. When children feel uncomfortable at a social situation, as often happens with a new experience, children tend to act out. If they feel confident that they can handle it, they can concentrate on having a good time. This kind of confidence builds more confidence.

Good manners will last a lifetime. They will be used on a child's first date. When a child grows up and gets married, the partner will appreciate the good social graces.

You might find that your eight-year-old is not fighting as much on the playground or is getting better grades and has more friends because he has learned how to take turns and say "Excuse me" or "I'm sorry." He will also learn that good manners have rewards. Even preschoolers will respond to magic words such as, "Excuse me."

The teacher will call on your child if he doesn't interrupt during instructions. Parents are inclined to allow him new privileges, such as going to a movie with a friend, or dad is more likely to take a child to a baseball game if he knows he can count on him to behave and use good manners.

What should you expect from your children at any given age? Raising polite children is to ask of them that which is is appropriate for their age level.

<u>Age three and four:</u>

● Say "please," "thank you," and "excuse me" with some prompting from you.
● Be able to eat in a restaurant, wait for food, and speak quietly in a public place.
● Become accustomed to having a napkin on their lap.
● Become acquainted with the idea of waiting until someone else has finished speaking before talking.
● Draw "thank you" pictures or dictate "thank you" notes.
● Say "hello," making eye contact with friends and grown-ups.
● Boys take their hats off in restaurants and in someone else's home.

Ages five and six:

- Expect your child to regularly say "please," "thank you," "excuse me," etc.
- Be able to wait for a restaurant meal without fidgeting and use an appropriate voice when speaking.
- Be able to place a napkin on their lap and use it. Keep elbows off the table while eating.
- Not interrupting others when they are talking.
- By age six ,write "thank you" notes; at age five, sign a "thank you" note written by an adult.
- Be able to greet people, and after visits say, "Thank you for coming." After visiting friends say, "Thank you for inviting me."
- Be able to answer the phone with a "Hello," and say, "I'll get my mother or father."
- Be able to chew food with mouth closed and don't try to talk while chewing.
- Be able to take hats off in a restaurant and hang them up in appropriate places.

Ages seven to ten:

- Has the habit of saying "Please," "Thank you," "Excuse me."
- Knows how to behave in a restaurant without being reminded.
- Has the habit of using a napkin properly.
- Knows how to carry on a conversation without interrupting.
- Is able to write their own than you note and say why they liked the gift.
- Is able to shake hands and make eye contact when greeting grown-ups and make some conversation.

● Is able to answer the phone, ask who's calling, and write
   down messages.
● Knows how to make proper introductions.
● Boys always take hats off in restaurants or someone's home
and in school buildings.

A child need to learn how
to behave in a restaurant
without being reminded.

Chapter Seven

VALUES START AT HOME

It is estimated that 10-15% of children in this county live in homes where the parents are teaching good values and social skills. Those are the ones we call the "good kids" in our community.

Values and social skills become part of the child's personality and are developed at an early age, before they start first grade. However, they need to be reinforced during their childhood. Young parents and grandparents are saying, "I don't have time to teach my kids." Because the parents are not teaching values, the federal government is hiring 200,000 police officers. Many states are building more and more prisons to accommodate the criminals in our society. The State of Oregon is building six new prisons.

When the family is teaching values, we need to say that mothers and fathers are equal, but different. Fathers have a different way of looking at the world. Fathers are more apt to play with the children. They take them camping, fishing, golfing, and fixing and doing projects that need to be done. Fathers are more apt to teach about what is right and wrong, fairness, respect, humor, courage, resourcefulness, responsibility, cooperation, and many more values.

A mother's love is her greatest gift to her children. It is mothers who teach good manners. "Johnny's elbows should be off the table." "I can understand you better when you don't have food in your mouth." Mothers are more apt to teach about caring, courtesy, patience, peace-making, empathy, and kindness.

Children tend to behave better in homes where there are two teaching parents, simply because they do have different roles in raising and teaching children important social skills and values. Good character is more to be praised than outstanding talent. Most talents are to some extent, a gift. Good character is not given; it is a learned trait.

Our democracy is based on laws that are intended to be just and to protect the majority of its citizens. That also applies to children at school. To be a successful student at school, children need to be able to obey the school rules. They simply need to know the difference between right and wrong, to be in control of their actions and to demonstrate proper behavior.

Parents need to teach children consistent standards of right and wrong in harmony with the culture, so that they may develop respect for themselves, members of the family, and the community.

Through the home, children begin to understand and practice the values of a democratic society with elected officials at all levels. They develop a good understanding of and respect for law and order. Also, children need to develop a concern for the welfare of others, as opposed to thinking only of themselves, which develops into selfishness. Here are some situations to discuss with your children:

Primary age child, grades K-3: John found a $10 bill on the floor near the teacher's desk. What should John do with the $10?

Intermediate age child, grades 4-6: What do you think is the most important thing in the world? (Avoid making judgments.)

<u>Upper grades</u>, 7-12: What does "justice" mean to you?

If you think your child's answer to these questions seems to indicate a skewed sense of right and wrong, then there are some things that you can do. You should have a standard set of rules for conduct, and be consistent. Children need to know that, if they break family rules, there will be consequences. You must make the consequences clear and enforce them every time. Accept no excuses. If you do accept excuses, then you are training your child to break the rules and make up excuses.

For older children, use newspaper articles to discuss moral problems and issues of right and wrong behavior. Avoid judgment statements, be a good listener and ask questions. Share what you might have done in a given situation.

For younger children, you might read *Aesop's Fables* and discuss the simple situations presented in the stories.

For the middle grades, you might have a discussion on the values of membership in character-building organizations such as Scouts, 4-H, church groups, school-sponsored organizations, Campfire, etc.

Encourage your child to be concerned for the welfare of others. Encourage volunteer service to the community, such as visiting senior citizens and doing chores for neighbors who may need assistance or help. All parents want their children to be responsible for their own behavior. You should want this responsibility to come from ultimate values, which are reverence for life and concern for human welfare. In other words, responsibility and values must be based on respect for life, liberty, and the pursuit of happiness.

Part of the problem is that values are hard to teach. They are rather absorbed and become part of the child through his identification with parents who give him a model from which to begin. Parents must accept the responsibility for teaching children values by their own example and behavior. The school is limited in what it can and should do concerning values. The question always comes up—whose values should the school teach?

HOW TO TEACH VALUES THROUGH HISTORY

Value Tales is a series of 26 books based on factual information, but presented in a fictional manner. They each tell of a well-known person's life and the moral value (honesty, perseverance) they best portrayed. The *Value Tales* series is a wonderful means of making history come alive in an extremely appealing fashion for even the youngest child.

Abraham Lincoln was well-known for his respect of all races of people. He fought to free the slaves and earned the respect of people everywhere for writing the Emancipation Proclamation and keeping the United States from dividing during the Civil War.

Thomas Jefferson excellently portrayed the value of foresight when he wrote the Declaration of Independence and founded the Democratic partly to help assure that the United States would never be ruled by a dictator. As founder of the University of Virginia, Jefferson also demonstrated his foresight for the value of education by extending the opportunities for education beyond public schools.

Eleanor Roosevelt, the wife of Franklin D. Roosevelt, is appropriately portrayed by the value of caring, which her life certainly reflected.

Your public librarian can assist you in finding the *Value Tales* or they can be purchased at a book store.

Children of all ages need good role models, especially when it comes to teaching values.

ONE REASON WHY CHILDREN LIE

My 12-year-old child lies to me. What can I do? Why do children lie? Occasionally children lie because they are not allowed to tell the truth.

When an older brother tells you that he hates his little brother, you may spank him for telling what he believes is the truth. So, he turns around and tells the obvious lie that he now loves his brother. You then reward him with a hug and a kiss. What is your son to conclude from such an experience? He could come to believe that the truth hurts, that dishonesty is rewarded, and that you love little liars!

If you want to teach honesty, then you must be prepared to listen to bitter truths as well as to pleasant truths. If you want your child to value honesty, then you must not encourage him to lie about his feelings, be they positive, negative, or even mixed feelings of love and hate. It is from your reactions that your child learns whether honesty is the best policy.

Consider this conversation:

Harry, 10, broke the bike given to him by his father. Harry hides the broken bike in the garage. Father finds the bike. Father asked these questions leading to conflict.

Father: " Where is your new bike?"

Harry: "It's somewhere."

Father: " I didn't see you riding it."

Harry: "Maybe someone stole the bike."

Father: "You're a liar! You broke the bike! Don't think you can get away with it. If there's one thing I hate, it's a liar."

Father gave him a spanking that will be long remembered.

Now, that was a battle that was not necessary. The father played detective and prosecutor. He would have been more helpful to his son by saying: "I see your new bike is broken. It did not last long. It's too bad. That was an expensive bicycle. Harry, I want you to help me and we'll fix your bike. Then I want you to take better care of your bicycle."

The boy learned an important lesson. "Father understands. I can tell him the truth about my troubles. I must take better care of my bike."

Your policy on lying should be clear. For instance, when you find a book that is overdue, simply state, "I see your library book is overdue."

Try to avoid questions, "Have you returned the book to the library? Are you sure? Then why is it still on your desk?"

Always try to make positive statements.

When your child's teacher tells you that your child failed the test, you should not ask questions such as: "Did you pass the test? Are you sure? Well lying won't help this time! We talked to your teacher and we know you failed miserably."

Instead, simply tell your child directly, "Your teacher told us you have failed the test. We are worried and wonder how we can help."

Avoid provoking a child into defensive lying or setting up opportunities for lying. When your child does lie, your reaction should not be anger and anxiety. You want your child to learn that there is no need to lie. Your teacher or school counselor may have more ideas. The library has many good books on dealing with lying.

BEING RESPONSIBLE

"I believe that every right implies a responsibility, every opportunity, an obligation, every position a duty."
—John D. Rockefeller, Jr.

Of all the values that parents must teach their children, responsibility is one of the most abstract for children to learn—the idea of taking responsibility for your words and actions. It is important that parents show children examples of responsible behavior through their own modeling. When you are modeling responsibility, explain to your child what you are doing and why. Be sure to make a connection between the benefits of being responsible and the well-being of the family.

Children as young as five years of age need to be taught to move beyond thinking about themselves and see the greater benefit which comes from good behavior. Children should learn to have empathy and to assume the role of others. This will give them an appreciation for others' feelings. Learning responsibility is needed to help the family live in harmony. Teaching children responsibility is essential to the family, to society, and to individual self-respect.

Being responsible means:

* Learning to behave so that one can be trusted by others.
* Contributing to the well-being of the family.
* Being able to feel what others might feel and to appreciate the needs of others in the family and society.
* Responding with the knowledge that the consequences are one's own to assume when a task is done or not done.
* Taking responsibility for our own actions.
* Considering the outcome and impact before saying or doing anything.

SHOWING KINDNESS

You can't always tell your kids to be kind to others, but if they see you doing it on a regular basis, it will rub off. Here are a few ideas on teaching kindness:

* Let your children observe you showing kindness to neighbors by shoveling their snow.
* Help an older person with groceries at the supermarket.
* Involve your children in taking prepared food to a sick friend or neighbor.
* Talk about people in your community who are doing good deeds and read heart-warming stories from the newspaper aloud.
* Acknowledge any acts of kindness your child initiates. Most parents share the same goal—to raise children who will contribute to the community and to the welfare of the family.

HAVING EMPATHY

"It is only with the heart that one can see rightly; what is essential is invisible to the eye."
—Antoine De Saint-Exupery

"Do unto others as you would have them do unto you." This is the rule so many learn as the "Golden Rule." It is one rule that must be taught if your children are to learn to live in peace with their neighbors, get along with their coworkers, and enjoy good relationships with family members and friends. Empathy is the building block of solid citizenship. With empathy, children become caring, compassionate human beings. It is as essential as air and water for our survival.

Parents should use discipline to teach children appropriate behavior. Use consistent, fair, and non-violent discipline for inappropriate behavior. This method uses empathy, understanding, and caring as the basis for its success, even in the face of children's sometimes unacceptable forms of behavior.

When your children misbehave, make sure they understand the consequences. State the problem very clearly and then drop it. You need to help your children understand the implications of their behavior while it is fresh in their minds. For example, "What you said to Sally hurt her feelings. I hope you wouldn't really want to hurt her." Children need to understand that what they say and do has lasting effects. You need to avoid focusing on the individual and point out the behavior.

What it means to have empathy:

* You can understand and assume the role of another person.
* Your child should be able to recognize and understand the emotions of others and then be able to share those emotions.
* Three-year-olds should have developed self-awareness, through which they will become capable of feeling and showing empathy for others. Empathy needs to be reinforced by the parents.
* As early as three years of age, children will show empathy when another is hurt and can recall when they have experienced similar hurts.
* To feel secure, infants should have strong bonds with at least their mother, so they will develop greater empathy for others as they grow and mature into adults.

Examples:

* "Dad! That must have hurt. Are you going to be all right?"

116

✳ "Mom, that's too heavy for you. Let me help you."
✳ "Dad is sick. Let's get his food and take it to him."
✳ "I learned so much about empathy from my parents and a little from my teachers. Empathy is so important."
✳ "To be understanding of another's feeling is a key to friendship."

BEING HONEST

"Living the truth in your heart without compromise brings kindness into the world. Attempts at kindness that compromise your heart cause only sadness."
—18th-Century Monk

It is the parents' responsibility to model honesty. It is difficult to expect children to always be honest if you cheat people, don't tell the truth, take advantage of others, or let a clerk give you too much change. The family is the best and almost the only teacher of honesty. Every decision you make is a model of living life honestly and compassionately.

You need to evaluate your own behavior and hold steady to being a model for honesty, even though you may be tempted to take an easier path than telling the truth. As you drive, obey the speed limit. Make sure that you are always honest in your daily dealings with others.

Up until about four years of age, children are usually honest because they don't understand dishonesty. Give your young children verbal rewards for doing an honest deed. When praising honesty, describe what your child did that was honest. Example: "I'm proud of you for putting your brother's toy back." Honesty needs to be supported continuously. As children get older, they see dishonesty daily—cheating on tests, telling little white lies, etc.

Honesty means being trusted by others and caring

117

enough to want to do the right thing. It means that you care about the rights of others and do not take advantage of other people. It is being respectable, having a good reputation ,and having honorable principles. You are truthful in sharing your thoughts and feelings.

❋ " Dad, I think that clerk gave you too much money. You shouldn't keep it."

❋ "I accidentally broke your best dish when I put popcorn in it for my friends. I'm sorry. Maybe I can find one like it and buy it with my baby-sitting money."

❋ "When people tell lies about other people, it just keeps going and going. Always tell the truth about another person. Then the lie will stop."

❋ "Honesty is a very important value because if your friends can't trust you, you won't have any friends."

BEING PATIENT

"You have to accept whatever comes, and the only important thing is that you meet it with courage and with the best you have to give."
—Eleanor Roosevelt

To help children develop patience and learn to tolerate frustration and adversity, it is important for them not to get their way all the time. They must experience low-risk struggles which force them to learn how to handle confusion and disappointment. When children are told they can't have something or that they have to delay getting what they want, they may throw a tantrum and demand that the world provide them with what they want, now!

Being patient means delaying wants till later. Planning for future goals requires that a child will be able to tolerate having to wait until later. Teach your children how to take the steps needed to reach goals. Understanding that we don't always get what we want and that we are not always entitled to everything is essential in developing patience.

❀ "Don't be so impatient. Your turn will come soon."
❀ "Mom, I'm O.K. I can get along without that expensive coat."
❀ "Mom, I'm so hungry, but I can wait until dinner is ready."
❀ "I didn't get a good grade on the history test. I guess I need to study harder for the next test."

BEING COURTEOUS

"Life is not so short that there is always time enough for courtesy."
—Ralph Waldo Emerson

Individuals who are considerate enough to think of the needs of others and to be courteous increase the pleasantness of everyday life and reduce its conflicts, which reduces the amount of violence we experience.

It usually happens that we are treated the way we treat others. This means that courtesy follows courtesy. It has been said that at school and in the work place, there seems to be a lack of courtesy.

Children are learning much of their social behavior from TV. It is vital for parents to monitor their children's TV viewing. It is important to watch what your children watch and discuss with them the lessons they may be learning.

Being courteous means:

✕ Having an awareness of the feelings of others.
✕ Engaging in smooth social interaction.

119

X Being courteous even when others are rude.
X Enjoying being civil to other people.

Examples:

X "Thanks for helping me with the groceries."
X "I got some money from Grandma and Grandpa. I want to get a card and send it to them."
X "Excuse me, I didn't know where the line was."

BEING LOYAL

> *"A friend is a person you give yourself."*
> —Robert Lois Stevenson

The first lesson in loyalty comes with the secure bonding between a baby and a caring parent. It is reinforced through those who create a sense of family for the young child. Only when children grow older do they begin to learn to care about other people at school, in the neighborhood, and in the community and to be willing to make some sacrifices for others.

Being loyal means:

X Keeping a promise that was made
X Caring about people enough to keep a commitment.
X Making sacrifices for the benefit of others.
X Allegiance to a greater cause.

Examples:

X "I know I'm not supposed to fight, but I couldn't let them hurt my friend."

✗ "Tomorrow is homecoming. I want to wear blue and gold, our school colors."
✗ "I'll get the assignment in tomorrow. I made a promise."

HAVING COURAGE

"Behold the turtle. He makes progress only when he sticks his neck out."
—James B. Connenet

Children and adults experience the pressures of "keeping up with the Joneses" and going along with the crowd. At school kids are teased. It takes courage to face the bully on the way home. Children are faced with difficult choices, requiring courage and conviction. To stand up to teasing, to stick to their family values and beliefs in spite of overwhelming pressure to go along with the crowd, to be unique when faced with not fitting in, to admit mistakes to others, all take courage.

Courage is best taught by the parents' own examples. Children want to behave as their parents do. When you are faced with frightening situations, it is important to show courage, so that your children can see how to handle their own fears.

Being courageous means:

✗ Taking some risks.
✗ Admitting that you made a mistake.
✗ Standing up for what you believe in.
✗ Having pride in being different.
✗ Standing up to teasing.

An eight-year-old said, " My dad taught me to be brave, but not dumb."

BEING A CARING PERSON

"The best portion of a good man's life. His little, nameless unremembered acts of kindness and of love."
—William Wadsworth

Infants and toddlers think primarily of themselves. They begin to care and to have empathy when the parents take care of their own needs, such as feeding them when they are hungry, changing their diaper, hugging them when they want to be hugged. When you do not teach caring to young children, they learn to be bullies, to demand from others, to become self-centered and to think nothing of unkindness, right or wrong—primarily because they haven't been taught otherwise.

Karen, an eight-year-old said, "Knowing that everyone has feelings makes it a lot easier to care about someone."

Being a caring person means:

✔ To be able to think about the needs and feelings of others.
✔ To be able to put yourself into the role of other people.
✔ To be able to experience empathy.
✔ To be able to defer your own needs and wants in order to help another person.

Caring is best taught by parents through behavior and actions. When Grandma says, "Nick, I'm going to make a casserole and take it to Dorothy and John. Dorothy is sick," Nick should go with Grandma to visit Dorothy. That's how caring is learned.

"I learned about caring when I was young. You have to be caring for others all your life. It also means taking care of pets, friends, parents, brothers and sisters, the plants in the house, and the garden."

BEING TOLERANT

"Toleration is good for all or it is good for none."
—Edmond Burk

Since we are living in an increasingly diverse world of work and play, the need for tolerance has never been greater. So many children begin to take the attitude that they are entitled to have anything they want, say, or do, whenever they want to say or do it. Some people don't want to make any effort to understand or accept others.

Tolerating frustration is being able to make the effort required to do things that are difficult. When children learn tolerance, they begin to understand the position of another person. They can appreciate the similarities and differences in people. The destructive nature of competition is reduced. Children can learn to lose without getting angry. Tolerance also means giving to others without expecting something in return.

Examples:

✔ "Grandpa, I hate peas, but I'll try some."
✔ "Kids were making fun of Sally because she is fat. I told everyone that was wrong."
✔ "My teacher doesn't like boys, but I guess I can put up with it."
✔ "I hate it when Nick goes into my room and looks around. I want some time by myself just to hang out when he isn't here in my room."

BEING FAIR

Johnny said, "Being fair is when you don't cut in front of someone in the lunch line. It is also taking turns at bat. My dad said, 'Being fair is part of living.'"

Fair: Is free from bias; being honest and just.

"Our deeds determine us, as much as we determine our deeds."
—George Eliot

Being fair may not mean treating everyone the same. Fairness is in the mind of the person. If fairness benefits only yourself, then many end up suffering. When we are really fair, we are able to get along with others because we are interested in everyone being treated fairly.One of the greatest compliments I received from one of my former students was, "Mr. Wonderley, you were always fair."

Being fair means:

✔ Going beyond the letter of agreement and rules to consider what is best for all.
✔ Believing that the needs and wants of others, as well as my own, are worth considering.
✔ Putting yourself in another person's place and working out a deal so that everyone feels they have been heard and everyone feels no one is being cheated.
✔ Caring about the welfare of others and beginning to overcome our own tendency to be selfish.

So that your children can better understand the idea of fairness, it is important for parents to watch their own behavior and to be as fair as possible with friends, neighbors, family members, store clerks, and those standing near you in waiting lines at the market. Make a point to discuss your fairness in working with other people so everyone feels like a winner.

SENSE OF HELPFULNESS

"Life's most persistent and urgent question is. What are you doing for others?"
—Martin Luther King, Jr.

Parents teach children to be helpful by saying; "Let me give you a hand! I'll take one end." "I think you need some help with that." "Let me help you with your homework."

When someone cries, "Help!" it is a signal of the importance of helping each other when in danger or in pain. We all feel better when we help someone. When children help others unselfishly, they experience a good feeling. When a person feels depressed, it always makes him feel better if he does a good deed for someone else.

Children need to learn, by your example, to put themselves in another person's place to see how others view things. Only then can your children learn how to live in harmony. The old story of the Little-Engine-That-Could will help children understand when someone offers to help, everything seems surmountable. Caring about the person being helped comes from a strong desire to please another person.

Being helpful means:

★ Giving without expecting anything in return.
★ Putting yourself in another person's position or role.
★ Transcending your own needs and thinking of the needs of others. This means acting from a base of caring and cooperation.

Your child begins to understand that the needs of others are to be considered along with her own. A third-grader said, "Being helpful means being nice to a new kid or showing a younger kid how to play hopscotch."

Children model parent behavior when one parent helps the other parent carry the groceries in, or when one parent opens the doors for the other and children hear, "Thank you for opening the door for me." Be sure to praise the thoughtful task rather than the child.

HAVING RESPECT

"True politeness is perfect ease in freedom. It simply consists in treating others just as you love to be treated yourself."
—Earl of Chesterfield

In order to respect others, you need to have self-respect. We all want to be treated with respect. When parents are teaching about respect, they have the responsibility to understand their children's point of view, even if they don't always agree with them. Through modeling of understanding and acceptance of others, a child will begin to learn to understand others. There is a need to think from another person's point of view, even if it is different from the child's own. Then children will learn to treat others with kindness and caring.

Children will begin to learn this lesson: to be respected, you must first respect. Children are more likely to find success in personal relationships when they learn to respect people they play and work with. When children learn to respect limits and have internalized boundaries that guide behavior, then they will be referred to as those "wonderful children." They can develop strong character, rather than developing alibis for the trouble they make.

Respect means:

★ Caring about the rights of others, even if they infringe upon

126

my own rights.
★ Thinking about another person in a positive way.
★ Caring about the feelings of others. We treat others the way we want to be treated.
★ Admiring another person's traits.
★ Having a good self-esteem demonstrates that we have self-respect.

Examples:

★ "I respect you for what you believe, but I'm not sure I can agree with you on that point."
★ "I wanted something from your room, but I didn't go in. I didn't want to invade your privacy."
★ "I didn't bring my new knife to school because I know it was against the rules."
★ "I'm sorry I offended you. I simply didn't think about how you might feel."

How do parents teach respect? I don't think a parent can teach respect the same way you teach a child to do math or to read. Respect for another person is best taught in a healthy family, where parents respect their children and children respect their parents and each other. All are not equal in terms of responsibilities and duties, but all are people, which does result in whole new ways of relating within the family. It is much more personal and less formal. This kind of respect is not superficial; it is real and deliberate.

Respect for others begins in the home, where individuals are respected for their uniqueness. If you show respect for your child, your spouse, and your friends, then your child will learn to respect others, even though all are different.

In our society, we have cultural disrespect. Cultural disrespect is the direct result of the unraveling of American society, with both parents working, and the extended family scattered rather than clustered in the same community, and with families organizing all types of child care arrangements.

Many of our kids are suffering from under-parenting, an absence of a positive male role-model due to divorce. Demanding work schedules mean that too many boys are growing up without a strong male presence to respect and emulate. Many have fathers who demonstrate derogatory attitudes toward women. Too many boys and girls are picking up ideas about girl-boy relationships from the "street." Many times boys learn from men that girls are just body parts and that sex is for fun, and all you need to do is wear the right protective gear.

Respect for others is best developed in a family that encourages children to play important roles in maintaining the welfare of their family. The greatest teaching tool you have is your own behavior. Here are some ways you can promote respect in your family:

▲ What you say and do will dictate the way your child speaks and acts towards others. If you tell your child, "You're a spoiled brat," then don't be surprised if your child tells a friend "You're ugly." Children who feel good about themselves are not going to hurt someone else either emotionally or physically.

▲ Monitor your own attitudes regarding gender roles. Do you encourage your son or daughter to be aggressive? Let talent, skills, and fairness determine gender roles—not whether your child is a boy or girl.

▲ Be careful not to give your children mixed messages. Keep in mind that your kids will do what you do, not what you say.

▲ Provide your son or daughter with positive role models. Boys learn what it is to be a male from the men in their lives. Girls learn how to be women from the women in their lives. Encourage your child toward relationships with his father, her mother, teachers, coaches, big brothers, big sisters, aunts and uncles, grandfathers and grandmothers.

▲ Don't tease your child about his body. Such comments will only teach your son or daughter to make hurtful remarks to others.

▲ Show your children how to communicate. Boys and girls need to be sensitive to what they say. Boys and girls need to learn by your example that they can't always anticipate how their behavior is going to affect someone and that it is their responsibility to ask, "Is it all right if_____?" or " Is it okay if_____?"

▲ Don't let sons or daughters generalize. By your example, teach your child that generalizations about any group of people—boys and girls, teachers, members of various races or religious beliefs—are wrong. Your child might be at an age when "girls are yucky" or "boys are all silly." Support their choosing of friends. Meanness should not be tolerated. There is no time when sexual harassment is a healthy development for your son or daughter.

Be sure you monitor your child's interaction with peers. Be sure your son or daughter understands "good" and "bad" touching and the privacy of people's bodies. Learn to communicate with your child about sex education, and communicate your values about sex, love, commitment, and appropriate relationships.

BEING COOPERATIVE

We cannot live only for ourselves. A thousand fibers connect us with our fellow men; among those fibers, as sympathetic threads, our actions run as causes, and they come back to us as effects."
—Herman Melville

The ultimate goal of living in a democratic society means its citizens are cooperative. Before children start kindergarten, if they have learned to be honest, to respect others, and to have empathy, they will be more apt to cooperate with others with whom they come in contact. Because they respect others, they can begin to put themselves in another's place and will treat others fairly. Children may not always do everything a person asks them to do. Concern for the welfare of others, as well as our own, makes cooperation work. Often there is a need for compromise.

Living in a family involves cooperation and sharing with other members of the family. To teach the importance of sharing, children need some rules, such as: whatever one has in his hands he may keep; when he puts it down, it becomes free for others to use. For older children and teens, this involves reinforcing their thinking about the needs of others and about what everyone will gain from an activity.

Being cooperative means:

▲ Working toward a common goal to benefit all.
▲ Developing a sense of higher duty, an obligation to the higher good.
▲ Understanding other people's viewpoint helps a person know how to cooperate with them.
▲ Each will need to compromise so that all can reach the goal.

130

▲ Everyone working together is the key ingredient for cooperation.

Examples:

❊ "I want to do my part by bringing a salad."
❊ "If we clean the house together, we can get it done quicker."
❊ "If we wash the car together, we'll have time to watch TV together."
❊ "Cooperation and compromise is important so we can have fun together later."

HAVING SELF-DISCIPLINE

"Self-reverence, self-knowledge, self-control. These three alone lead life to sovereign power."
—Lord Tennyson

Without house rules, it is difficult for parents to teach self-discipline. Children are torn between having fun now and doing tasks later. Self-discipline is the heart of living a life of self-reliance and self-sufficiency. Children are faced daily with the dilemma of having fun versus the satisfaction of a task completed.

Children need rules in their lives to help govern their behavior. As an adult, your life is full of rules. Rules for children's behavior tells children what you want them to do, rather then what you don't want them to do. Example: "I want you to put your dirty clothes in the hamper." "I want you to come when you are called."

One mother posted rules for all to see on the bulletin board in the kitchen:

Rule #1. Do wait your turn.

Rule #2. Do come when called.
Rule #3. Do get along with your brother.
Rule#4. Do chew with your mouth closed.
Rule#5. Do leave a toy alone if someone else is playing with it.

What it means to have self-discipline:

❋ Setting goals and working toward them.
❋ Being able to postpone fun for the greater good.
❋ Making up your mind about the boundaries for behavior and respecting the boundaries of others.
❋ Understanding and projecting yourself into another person's place.
❋ Having a set of internal frames of reference rather than external control: adult-demonstrated self-control.

Examples:

❋ "I decided not to hit my brother because I remember the rule."
❋ "What is the rule about toys?"
❋ "Playing here is fun because there are rules."
❋ "When you're self-disciplined you are much more independent and organized."

HAVING A SENSE OF HUMOR

"Humanity takes itself too seriously. It is the world's original sin. If the caveman had known how to laugh, history would have been different."
—Oscar Wilde

SUCCESS STARTS EARLY!

Infants are able to laugh with joy at moments of discovering and learning. Sometimes children lose sight of the value of laughter and humor when they feel unloved and when their lives lack the influence of parents who show them how to spice up life with a good sense of humor. To be able to see the humor in life requires an appreciation of its spontaneity and its mistakes. Humor is best taught in the context of a caring and supportive home, encouraging feelings of happiness and a sense of wonder about the world and solving adversity rather than looking for someone to blame.

Good humor means:

■ Finding humor in everyday living and not taking life too seriously.
■ Involves believing in oneself.
■ Having a creative view of our imperfect world.
■ Accepting life as it is can be an element of humor.

Examples:

■ "Always laugh with someone, not at them."
■ "Mistakes are easier when you can see the funny side."
■ "I like to date boys who have a good sense of humor."

Recently, a concerned parent said, "My child never laughs at anything funny." As parents, we all should be concerned. Humor and laughter are good for all of us. It is said that "laughter is good medicine."

Being a good parent is serious business. Many parents are afraid they will fail in their job as parents. What you really need to do is relax and enjoy your children and not be so intent on doing a good job. Your good examples for your children are really the best message. If you have your own "act" together, you really don't have too much to worry about. If we don't

133

enjoy our children, surprisingly, they may not enjoy us either.

Families need to find time to laugh together. CAUTION: Don't laugh at your child, laugh with him.

When we take time to recapture a sense of fun and humor, we can make disaster less devastating and stress easier to tolerate. We can turn those lousy days into good ones. Nurses tell us that laughter helps people heal faster. They are happier and feel better.

You might try using some tricks that others have tried with success, such as:

- When toys needed picking up, one father used a robot voice, "This is BS-10, your robot speaking. My walking field needs clearing or my circuits will jam. Beep beep." In seconds the young child cleared the floor of toys. The child could see the sense of humor in the unusual request.
- A parent made up a humorous limerick to post on a son's bedroom door on his return from school. Then the son posted an original limerick to his mother's door.
- A six-year-old vegetable-hater began eating peas after they were called Martian heads.

Find time each week for fun. Play board games designed for families. Read some of Mark Twain's short stories aloud. Take time to walk together and enjoy each other. Learn to laugh at your silly mistakes. Rediscover the joy of play.

Humor should be used with caution. Remember to always laugh with your children, not at them. When we laugh at them, it becomes ridicule and sarcasm, which is not appropriate. If your child feels embarrassed or attacked, you need to re-evaluate your approach.

We parents and grandparents do have a serious job of properly raising children to be happy, responsible, reasonably obedient, knowledgeable, and competent to live and work independently.

BEING TRUSTWORTHY

> *"What you deny others will be denied to you, for the plain reason you are always legislating for yourself, all your words and actions define the world you want to live in."*
> —Thaddeus Golas

Babies learn to trust their mothers to feed them, change their diapers, and pick them up when they need to be picked up and cuddled. They develop strong bonds with the mother the first year of life by trusting that an adult will take care of their needs.

This trust bonding with the mother will last the rest of their lives and affect how they deal with other people as they get older.

As children grow older, they see adults doing things that they are required to do. When teaching about trustworthiness, it is vital to show them daily how adults can be depended upon. When you make promises, keep them, be on time, carry out promises, and let them see you follow through with your plans, unless you have an honest reason for changing.

What it means to be trustworthy:

❧ Caring about the needs of others.

❧ Having self-respect and believing that the opinions of others count.

❧ Making an effort to keep promisse and developing a reputation for being trustworthy.

❧ Ensuring that people will trust you to do what you say you will do.

135

Examples:

- ☝ "I'll get my chores done before I go outside to play."
- ☝ "Scott, I know I can trust you with the car."
- ☝ "I trust you. I know you will pay me back."
- ☝ "I always feel honored when my friends put their trust in me."

BEING MOTIVATED

> *"The purpose of life is a life of purpose."*
> —Robert Byrne

The family who develops self-motivated children has rules that guide them in their daily lives. Children need rules for living so they will know what is expected of them. When developing rules, state the rules in terms of what you want your children to do, rather than what you don't want them to do. Rules that are stated as "do" rules, give children a guide for behavior. When the rules are house rules, they are enforced even when grandparents, baby-sitters, or friends are designated managers.

Examples:

- ❖ "The couch is for sitting; the floor is for your feet with shoes on."
- ❖ "In this house we always close the door when we come in or out."

When setting goals, parents need to help children set reasonable long and short-term goals and help them go through the steps to accomplish these goals. Children need to have assigned tasks. Help them go through each step. "Put a plate on the table for each person and then the silverware." It might help if your child watches you do it first. With your older children, have the child help you wash the car, and then the next time, assign the task.

Rewarding tasks completed promptly and correctly is important. Avoid giving praise to the child. Rather give praise for a task completed.

For example, " The table looks nice. Now we can all sit down to a nice meal." "Scott, the car looks clean and ready to go." Avoid giving tangible rewards for a task. They'll learn to do chores only if there are material rewards. Doing a good job needs to be an internal satisfaction rather than an external reward, such as money, stickers, food, or the like.

Self-motivation means:

❖ To respond to internal rewards that direct children toward their goals.
❖ Having self-respect.
❖ Being self-driven, which is an internalized set of rules and boundaries.
❖ Being able to respond to the intrinsic reinforcement of an activity rather than to always need external reinforcement.

Examples:

❖ "I have this term paper to do. I'm going to get started on it now so I won't panic."
❖ "When I do my homework before I go out to pay, I can play without worrying."
❖ "I like my room better when it is cleaned up."
❖ "Dad, I want to get up early in the morning so I can study again for the history test."
❖ "I'm self-motivated because I get my homework done without being told."

BEING SELF-RELIANT

> *"No bird soars too high, if he soars with his own wings."* —William Blake

When children are allowed to watch too much TV, they become dependent on being entertained by others in situations in which they don't have to lift a finger to play games. This dependency can be hard to overcome and does lead to lower reading scores.

When children learn to be creative, they will always be blessed with inner tools of self-reliance. To be self-reliant, children must be given the freedom to express their thoughts and feelings and must receive positive feedback for taking risks. Avoid giving any kind of tangible reward for being self-reliant.

Limit primary-age children to one hour of TV daily, and older children to two hours. This will give them time to be creative, to play learning games, read books, and the play games with friends.

Being self-reliant means:

* Having pleasant associations with activities that are self-generated.
* Being controlled by forces from within rather than by those of the environment.
* Using one's own creativity and imagination.
* Activities promoting self-reliance should be present and should cost very little.

Examples:

* "I enjoy playing with my dolls. I'm playing house."
* "I enjoy reading books; I learn so much."

∗ "You are having a lot of fun playing by yourself."
∗ "I always have something to do. Watching TV is not intelligent."

BEING RESOURCEFUL

"If the only tool you have is a hammer, you tend to see every problem as a nail."
—Abraham Maslow

By four years of age children become resourceful in solving problems. When preschoolers play with toys, they encounter problems which must be solved on their own. Many parents would like to shield their children from life's disappointments by solving all problems for them. Children want to be independent. The more practice they get solving problems at an early age, the better. The wise parent knows when to give assistance.

What parents desire in their children is to develop skills in problem-solving, so they will become self-sufficient and self-reliant when they reach adulthood.

Being resourceful means:

∗ To become independent and self-sufficient, problem solving must be learned.
∗ That problem-solving involves a set of skills that can be learned, practiced, and refined.
∗ Problems may be barriers that prevent people from reaching their goals, but they learn alternative ways to reach them.
∗ Problem solving has its limitations. Individual power must be recognized.

Examples:

* ✱ "I got mad at my boyfriend, but we worked it out."
* ✱ "I couldn't solve this algebra problem, so I found one like it and solved the problem."
* ✱ "You have to be smart to solve hard problems, I think patience is an important part. The answer might be simpler than you thought."

When children act independently, they are demonstrating their ability to be resourceful. Sometimes parents discourage independence because they think they will not be able to reach their goal. Children should be encouraged to attempt to do things on their own, even though they may fail. Your job is to be encouraging. Failure is a way of learning and problem solving.

Section Four

> *A hundred years from now, it will not matter what my bank account was, the sort of house I lived in, or the kind of car I drive—but the world may be different because I was important in the life of a child.*
>
> —Kathy Davis

Chapter Eight

PUTTING YOUR CHILDREN FIRST

Parenting is the art of bringing up children without putting them down. Do you expect your family to be gracious and understanding and to show kindness to others? Or do you hear everyone complaining and grumbling? Can you be flexible or are you rigid?

To grow up healthy and happy and to be good students, children need parental time and attention. Who will help 10-year-old John deal with the agony of not having been invited to a classmate's birthday party? Who will help 16-year-old Jimmy have good values when he begins to date? Who will help 17-year-old Jane cope with being cut from the ball team? A parent, of course. But if neither parent is at home at 4 p.m. or 6 p.m., how would a parent even know that these things are troubling their children?

Since the 1960s, children have lost 12 hours of parental time per week, and research has pointed to the link between absentee parents and a large range of emotional and behavior problems. A study conducted in 1989 surveyed 5,000 eighth-grade students in California. It found that the more hours children were left alone after school, the greater the risk of drug abuse.

Why has good parenting become such a struggle in recent years? Why has parenting become such a thankless task? Why are some adults finding it hard to put families and children first?

Part of the answer is in the way our culture has tilted toward the "self" movement. The liberation movement of the sixties greatly increased the weight men and women give to self-gratification and has had negative effects on how we treat children. These are trade-offs between personal gratification and family well-being. Creating a home and raising children are time-consuming activities which take up large amounts of parents' energy in the prime of their lives. It is energy that cannot be spent on advancing a career.

Both government and business can do many things to give parents the wonderful gift of time with children. For example, one company offers a compressed work week. Employees are able to work 40 hours in three or four days. Other businesses are offering flexible work weeks, so parents can spend more time with children. Both companies find that these options for working parents boost productivity.

Employers, parents, and the community all must work together, so that parents can spend more time with their children. No longer can society afford to put children at risk. Parents need the time to teach children the values they need to stay out of trouble.

SOCIETY'S ILLS CAN BE TRACED TO FAMILY BREAKDOWN

Recently, I was at a committee meeting where the subject of vandalism came up. Various ideas surfaced about why we have so much vandalism in our society. We talked about graffiti on public buildings, shot-up road signs, paintings on national monuments, the destruction public property.

Why? Some said it is done just for the fun of it. For whatever reason, it has become such a serious problem that our U.S. Congress is debating a crime bill and plans to spend several billions on stopping crime. There's only one thing the federal government can do to help stop crime. That is to help support the family so that there is a father and mother teaching children traditional family values.

What we do need are homes that teach children moral values, the difference between right and wrong, good manners and good social skills. I've discussed the problem of vandalism with people who deal with the young people who get into trouble with the police. They tell me we have a whole generation of parents who were not taught traditional family values in the home.

* We now have a generation of adults raising children who did not respect public property themselves.
* People who vandalize and commit crimes have a low self-esteem. Graffiti is a statement of anger within the individual. Their message is "I'm not important." Kids will do anything to get attention, even if it is negative attention, which is punishment. In the classroom it is called "acting out." Children receive some attention, even if being sent to the principal for poor behavior.
* Children who are raised in nurseries seem to learn to be "mean." They are not getting the motherly love and affection they need to grow up loving and caring, with the self-respect that only an unhurried mother can provide— a mother who was also loved by her mother.
* A recent Gallop Poll found that 70 percent of Americans agree with the statement, "The most significant problem facing the American family is the physical absence of the teaching father from the home."

Former Vice-president Dan Quayle said it best when he stated, "Children need love and discipline. They need mothers and fathers. A welfare check is not a husband. The state is not a father. It is from parents that children learn to behave in society; it is from parents above all that children come to understand values and themselves as men and women, mothers and fathers."

Then he added: "It's time to talk about family, hard work, integrity, and personal responsibility. We cannot be embarrassed out of our belief that two parents, married to each other, are better in most cases for children than one. That honest work is better than hand-outs or crime. That we are our brother's keepers, that it's worth making an effort, even when the rewards aren't immediate."

I believe there are some things we can start doing to get our kids back on the right track:

* We need to stop putting a stamp of approval on having children out of wedlock.
* Being a mother should be honored in our society. Being a mother is not a part-time venture. Young children need to be raised by loving, caring mothers, rather than by the TV where young children can't make a distinction between fact or fiction.
* We need to send the entertainment industry a message that every child needs both a mother and a father and they both have their functions in raising happy, healthy and responsible children.
* Until we fix our families, vandalism and crime will continue to increase. More police, more welfare, is not a solution. I believe that churches in every community have the knowledge, the resources to make a big difference. Churches are the one institution that can help put the family back together.

PROMISES FOR BETTER PARENTING

Decide now to work toward improving the quality of your family life. Here are some areas you may want to work on:

* Promise to spend more time with your children. Even 16-year-old kids need your time.
* Promise to read to or listen to your children read every day.
* Promise to go to the library with your children and be sure every child has a library card. Have planned reading time every day with the TV and radio turned off.
* Promise to give your children new and quality learning experiences to increase their knowledge and vocabulary.
* Promise to say something positive to your children to help build self-esteem. This will help your children behave better and like themselves better.
* Promise to support your children's schools and, especially, their classroom teachers, so they will behave better and get a better education and the teachers will not have to spend their time on discipline.
* Promise to spend five minutes every day listening to each child. Sharpen your listening skills, so you will know what is going on in their lives.
* Promise to provide a learning environment in your home where each child can do homework without being disturbed by TV, siblings, or friends.
* Promise to have high standards for good behavior. Use good manners and have agreed-upon consequences for non-compliance.
* Promise to show your children how to be a good friend so they will have good friends.
* Promise to give your children security and love, so they will

be happy and will like themselves and will be liked by others.

* Promise to monitor and limit the amount of TV programs your children watch, so they will have time to read, do homework, and work on hobbies.
* Promise to make sure your children get a balanced diet, plenty of sleep, and exercise so they can have the energy needed to get maximum benefits from classroom instruction.

TIME TOGETHER

There are so many activities that keep families from spending good, quality time together. Children are better students when the family spends time together, when parents are able to listen to them and take an active role in their learning experience.

This checklist will help you decide how your family is doing:

* Do you see your kids enough, or are you so busy that you see them on the run? Is your schedule and lifestyle so hectic that you want to scream?
* Does your family have meals together? It has been demonstrated that children in families that eat together had greater reading proficiency. Eating dinner together provided an opportunity for discussion to occur and thereby promoted listening skills and expressive oral language.
* Is your life over-scheduled and hectic? Will all this running to this meeting and that meeting, rushing to little league, rushing to scouts for another kid, then rushing to another meeting leave you with enough time for family get togethers? Will all this running around make that much difference 20 years from now? Sit down with your kids

and have an honest discussion about priorities.

* Are you sending your kids to school clean and well-groomed? I frequently see kids going to school in clothes that are dirty. Their hair is dirty, and they are wearing clothing that is really not appropriate. I've worked with kids and have been confused as to whether the child was a boy or a girl. For children to have good mental health, they need to dress appropriately.

* Are you neglecting your teenage children? Just because your teenager is 5 feet 8 inches and growing doesn't mean she doesn't need your influence and supervision. You need to trust your teenagers, but at the same time know where they are and what kind of activities they are involved in. You need to have the time and patience to listen to your teenager every day for at least five minutes without being judgmental. That five minutes is probably the most important five minutes you will every spend. It will pay off now and later. Your teenager will learn to confide in you and seek your advice.

* Do you have time to encourage leisure reading in your home? Be sure you have the energy and time and are not too stressed out to let your kids see you enjoying pleasure reading. Do you read to your preschooler?

With modern gadgets in the home and so much pressure for our time, it is wise for all parents to reevaluate their busy schedules. Many teachers are concerned that children are being neglected. Children who are neglected frequently demonstrate disruptive behavior, low reading scores, and low self-esteem.

MEALTIME IS TIME FOR FAMILY CONVERSATION

Meal conversation improves language development. The family gathering around the dinner table has long been a part of American culture. Now, families seem to be too busy to eat together. All family member are going their own way.

Harvard's Graduate School of Education and Clark University's Education Department have done research showing that eating meals together is important for more than sentimental reasons. Table conversation helps build literacy.

When parents of preschoolers read to their children and then stop to interpret what they read; when parents take children on outings where they hear new vocabulary terms; and when they play fantasy games with children or engage them in mealtime talk that goes beyond, "Please pass the salt and pepper," they provide opportunities for children to exercise a variety of oral language skills.

These are the kinds of skills, which the researchers call "decentralized" language abilities, that come from children's exposure to talk that goes beyond the here and now and relies more heavily on the words themselves to give a clearer picture for the listener. Children who often engage in conversation become skilled at speaking (expressive oral language). For example, they are good at reporting on an event to someone who was not there, telling a story, defining words, and using new and varied vocabulary when they talk.

The researchers report that there is a link between table conversation between family members and children's literacy success later on in school. Reading involves much more than just "sounding out" words. It is understanding what is being read: complex comprehension skills. These are expressive oral language skills that require practice. It's not that these oral language skills are so difficult or so inaccessible, but the child must develop fluency in expressive oral language.

Most research on children's literacy in the past has focused on how children acquire phonetic skills and the ability to "sound out" words and a large number of pre-reading skills such as the ability to recognize that print is read from left to right. Little attention has been given to expressive oral language skills and how they contribute to the complex interplay that reading is.

The amount of conversation taking place during mealtime is linked to children's abilities in the primary grades—to understand stories and to learn new words. Mealtime conversation improves children's vocabulary.

The research clearly makes a strong case for explaining why families eating meals together is critical to the overall language development of young children. Mealtime offers opportunities for children to hear new words, to negotiate their turn to speak, and to recount the events of the day for family members who were not there.

The bottom line is that children benefit from lots of adult talk. They also develop a multitude of important social skills that are needed to function at school and in the work place.

THE TEN COMMANDMENTS FOR MODERN PARENTS

1. Give your children the support of your love, confidence, and appreciation for their individuality.
2. Plan for good times with your children. Try always to realize how things seem to a child, and make an effort to support your children's' school activities.
3. Give your children a share in the tasks and creative activities of the home.
4. Look for good in your children for which you can praise

more than for faults which you must condemn. Learn to be positive in your own life.

5. Learn to value curiosity in your children and stimulate in them the love of all things true and beautiful.
6. Teach your children to convert obstacles into opportunities for improvement.
7. Develop in yourself those qualities which you want your children to have. They will do what they see you do.
8. Make your home a center of friendship, good neighborliness, and compassion for others.
9. Share with your children the fellowship of your faith, and make an effort to live your faith.
10. Help your children know the difference between right and wrong and develop by example the values of honesty, truthfulness, and fair play.

LISTENING IS A PARENTING SKILL

The old saying, "Children should be seen and not heard," was never a good parenting practice. Children who are not listened to in the home live in a lonely silence. You, the parent, will not know what they are feeling, how they are coping, or what they are doing.

Recently a teenager admitted that the neatest thing about his father was, "He always listened to me." The father told me later, "I wasn't aware that listening to my son was so important to him. My parents listened to me," he said, "so it was just natural for me to listen to my son." This particular father and son did things together, and there was mutual respect between them. The father listened to his son and never ridiculed or made fun of him in public or in private.

All children need parents who have the time and will take the time to spend with their children and listen with understanding and respect. They will not talk to you, if what they say is not valued or respected. The greatest gift that you can give a child is to be with him—stop what you are doing and just listen.

Those who counsel others tell me that the most important thing we do is to listen to people without judging. Being able to talk freely and have someone listen with understanding can be one of the most therapeutic things in our lives.

Listening to your children helps them in so many ways. First of all, it is a direct way of showing love. Your children are new in this world. They experience fear, sadness, and loneliness. They have so much to learn from you. When they are part of a good parent-child relationship, they receive a strong sense of reassurance in living. They feel less alone in growing up. They are assured that someone else who cares is there.

When you treat your children with respect, you are setting an example for them to follow. Your children will meet life with the same complicated abilities to experience, feel, and think. They'll make judgments from their own understandings. They'll make choices and act upon those choices based on their judgments. When you take the time to listen, you are conveying to them that they are valued and respected. Children need to be able to trust themselves to deal with experiences and conflicts they will face. It is this kind of faith that your children need to move into the world, knowing that they are okay and that they can effectively deal with whatever comes their way.

Listening brings about such powerful healing! It can be the most beautiful, important gift that parents can give their children.

BONDING IS ESSENTIAL

The ability to trust, love, and to respond to love begins with motherly love during infancy and early childhood. It is then nurtured through the school years. According to many studies, the inability to love results from the absence of bonding during those crucial early years.

Early bonding is essential to develop trust within the child. When the infant cries because it is hungry, needs a diaper changed, or wants to be cuddled, it needs to know someone is there. This quality of sensitive care by the mother develops a sense of personal worthiness within the child.

In the late 1970s, not much was known about the mother/infant bond and its effects on later life. What does a child need in order to feel the world is a positive place and that she has value? It is estimated that more than a third of American children suffer from weak bonding with their mother. School-age children thus afflicted may exhibit hostile behavior, such as bullying and other aggressive acts or become loners or victimized by other children.

Magid and McKelvey, in their book *High Risk Children Without Consciences,* report that many adults forming weak ties with parents became robbers, thieves, drug pushers, or prostitutes. Where there was no bonding, it wasn't uncommon for adults to become murderers, sadists, and serial killers.

The Conscience of Humanity

Chart used permission of Bantam Books.

153

Conversely, children with strong bonds tend to become good marriage partners and humanitarians.

What can parents do to ensure a strong bond with their children?

❧ During infancy a parent should be home giving the child the emotional setting which establishes basic bonds and trust. This requires the continuous presence of a parent or permanent baby-sitter, one upon whom the child can depend and feel protected. Once basic bonding or trust has been established, it must be nurtured throughout the entire period of the child's school years.

❧ Mother should talk face-to-face with her infant. All you need to do is to sit down and hold your baby so you can make eye-to-eye contact and then begin talking. This is vital to developing both strong bonds and a strong intellect.

❧ Reading to your baby daily develops strong bonds, intelligence, and listening skills. The mother's reading voice is also very soothing to the child.

❧ Singing lullabies also improves bonding and intellect. Singing is a most calming activity for you and your baby.

❧ An infant's brain is like a computer. It stores words for use later. Mothers need to talk to their children when they take them on walks, while they change their diapers, and while they feed them.

BASIC NEEDS

For children to be happy and to do their very best in school, there are some very basic needs which I feel are very important. Your child needs to be healthy and strong and to have good food, plenty of sleep, exercise, and lots of fresh air.

They have other needs as well. Dr. Harry Smallenberg states that every child needs and requires:

* Love. Every child needs to feel that his parents love, want, and enjoy him; that he matters very much to someone; that there are people near him who care what happens to him.
* Acceptance. Every child needs to believe that his parents like him for himself, just the way he is; that they like him all the time and not only when he acts according to their ideas of the way a child should act; that they always accept him, even though they may not approve of the things he does; that they will let him grow and develop in his own way.
* Security. Every child needs to know that his home is a good, safe place; that his parents will always be on hand, especially in times of crisis when he needs them most; that he belongs to a family or group; that there is a place where he fits in.
* Protection. Every child needs to feel that his parents will keep him safe from harm; that they will help him when he must face strange, unknown and frightening situations.
* Independence. Every child needs to know that his parents want him to grow up and that they encourage him to try new things; that they have confidence in him and his ability to do things for himself and by himself.
* Faith. Every child needs to have a set of moral standards to live by; a belief in the human values of kindness, courage, honesty, generosity, and justice.
* Guidance. Every child needs to have friendly help in learning how to behave; grownups around him who show him by example how to get along with others.
* Control. Every child needs to know that there are limits to what he is permitted to do and that his parents will hold him to these limits; that though it is all right to feel jealous or angry, he will not be allowed to hurt himself or others when he has these feelings.

155

When children's basic needs are satisfied, they have a better chance to grow up with good mental health and to become good students who are more apt to work up to their potential. They will be able to be on task at school, they will feel like doing their homework, and they will be interested in learning. I also believe that, if children's basic needs are met, they will be able to maintain healthy friendships. They will grow up to be good parents, good mates, good workers, good neighbors, and good citizens.

ALL CHILDREN NEED SECURITY AND TRUST

Security in the home is a basic need for both adults and children, says child psychologist Dr. Anita Stafford. Frequently, adults can and will express their frustrations with a lack of security, but a child only expresses anxiety or poor behavior. Parents must be willing to listen with understanding to their children. Adults' needs for security are basically the same as their children's. We can frequently express our feelings, but we do not always understand why we feel the way we do.

Child psychologists tell us that the child learns as an infant about trust and mistrust. For example, when a child cries, the mother's keen sense of hearing tells her the baby needs her. The baby's keen sense of hearing tells him that the sound of the footsteps are bringing relief to her need for food or a diaper change. Therefore, the complicated need for security is being met. The infant is developing a feeling of trust.

I am constantly amazed at how early parents can communicate with their child. What if the mother does not respond to the child's cry and take care of the child's discomfort? Then, mistrust and a strong feeling of insecurity soon develop, and problem behavior may be the end result. Of course, an adult who is experiencing problems in marriage or on the job is going to feel the same insecurity. However, adults, through experience, know how to handle those feelings. Too often, that adult feeling is transmitted to the child, who may not understand.

The following are a few things that parents can do to help children feel more secure:

* Have meals on time.
* Provide time for playing with friends.
* Read to your child at a regular time, just before bedtime.
* Provide a time for television viewing for the family.
* Be on time to avoid keeping your child waiting for you. One minute can seem like an eternity to an anxious child.
* Always do what you say or promise a child. You can teach your child to be dependable by being dependable.
* Take time each day to listen to your child with understanding.
* Always use positive directions, such as, "I want you to walk in the house." When we scream, "Don't run in the house!" this is a nondirective statement which does not give you the desired results. The directive should have previously understood consequences. It is better to say, "You can run outside, but walk in the house."

If you are going to help children become more secure, then you need to establish a more secure self. All adults feel more secure when they have a set routine. A husband comes home at a set time every day. Dinner is always at the same time. We can trust that it will happen at the same time every day. We do need to be flexible, however, when something goes wrong.

Try to be a caring adult by being prompt, since we are all dependent upon someone else. Develop your own listening skills when communicating with other adults, so there can be clear communication. One of our basic needs is to have the security that someone will listen. Practice positive comments when talking with others, as positive feelings help make you feel more secure.

If a child lives with security, he learns to have faith.

FOUR THINGS YOU SHOULD KNOW ABOUT RAISING YOUR CHILDREN

If you want your children to grow to be responsible, happy, and well-adjusted, there are four things that are essential.

1. <u>You love them no matter what goes wrong</u>.
   That is called unconditional love. Your children can depend on you. If your teenage daughter got pregnant, would you help her through this difficult time? If your son was drunk and wrecked the family car, would you help him out? Do your children know that, beyond a shadow of a doubt, you would come and get them, no matter what? That is what unconditional parental love is all about—like the shepherd who left the flock and got one lamb that had wandered away.

2. <u>You believe in them</u>.
   You believe in them no matter what. When they have made a mistake and you come to help them, do they know they must face consequences for their actions? Many abused children believe that their parents do not care for them when they are placed in foster homes. Do your children know they are a blessing to you?

3. <u>You discipline them consistently</u>.
   Adults who work with abused children report that children want discipline. Sometimes parents are afraid to disci-

pline, because they fear their children won't love them afterward. Parents make the mistake of making threats of punishment for misbehavior but never seem to carry them out. Kids soon learn they can get away with things because their parents "don't care." Children begin to believe that a broken promise is a lie. If you promise that a child will be punished for doing something wrong, then you had better do it. Your child will test you to see if you are going to keep your promise. Teenagers who go through the court systems report that their parents were not consistent. They would make threats of punishment but never carry through.

4. Don't give up.

Children who get into trouble complain to counselors that their parents should not have given up. Many children have a hard time forgiving their parents for not trying hard enough. I was told about a father of a 14-year-old boy who had thrown up his hands. "I don't know what I'm going to do," he said. One angry girl said, "I hate golf because my dad loved hitting golf balls at the driving range more than he loved me." The average father spends about four minutes a week in conversation with his children. Divide that time in half if the child has anything to say. Most dads are using their time to lecture and not listen. Lecturing to children has no value. Only active listening makes a difference.

Children want to be listened to. Children want discipline. Children want structure and order. Give your children these four essential gifts.

ONE-TO-ONE COMMUNICATING

With teenagers, you will probably have to start the conversation. It is in these unplanned, informal times that they are most likely to open up on the difficult and hurting topics that are bothering them. If both of you are not comfortable just talking casually, where and when will you find the time and place to bring up those tough topics? If you have a good track record with your children, they will feel secure in expressing their fears, doubts, and disappointments.

In the process of this one-to-one communication, you will be able to know what is going on in your teen's daily life. You will know when a need must be met *now*. You will be alerted to step in and take action in the most appropriate way.

I know a parent who took the advice to listen to her daughter for 10 minutes every day. This mother said, "I always knew how she was doing, how school went, who her friends were, and what was bugging her."

The girl is now in college and is on the dean's list. This mother felt that listening to her daughter for a few minutes every day was the most valuable thing she did.

GOOD HEALTH

If your child's health is a problem, then you are not alone. National studies estimate that 20 to 30 percent of children in school, ages 5 to 18, lack good health to the degree that it affects their academic progress and contributes to poor behavior at home and at school. If by chance your child is one of the 20 to 30 percent with poor health and you can admit it, you have solved 50 percent of the problem.

Here are some characteristics that distinguish healthy children from those who are not healthy. Some of these characteristics can affect learning, behavior, the intellectual development, and the physical development of your child.

● <u>Has energy</u>. My child is able to carry out routine activities at home and to complete chores and do homework without undue fatigue.

● Enjoys playing. My child is able to play with other children and participates in physical activities.

● Is coordinated. My child demonstrates skills in games and uses large and small muscles appropriate for age and sex.

● Growing normally. My child shows progressive gains in weight and height without unusually wide deviation.

● Interested in learning. My child has enough energy to do the things that most children of her age want and should do.

● Appetite. My child's appetite is good and she eats nutritional foods.

● Takes part in group activities. My child is interested in and is enthusiastic about activities that are popular with her age group.

● Social skills. My child has confidence in her own abilities, yet enjoys working and playing with others.

● Self-control. My child is able to show self-control in most situations.

● Rested. My child appears to have enough sleep to be alert and gets enough sleep for her age.

● Vision. My child holds a book at an appropriate distance and does not squint when reading or writing.

● Hearing. My child does not habitually fail to respond when called on or turn one ear toward the person talking.

● No colds. My child does not have frequent colds or persistent nasal discharge.

● Skin. My child does not have rashes or inflamed skin areas and is not frequently scratching.

● Coordinated. My child does not have more accidents than are typical of her age.

● Dental. My child does not complain of a toothache or sore or bleeding gums and does not have excessive tartar on teeth.

● Sores on mouth. My child does not have frequent sores in

161

or around the mouth and does not have cracking lips.
- <u>Self-concept.</u> My child appears to be happy and likes himself.
- <u>Others like my child</u>. My child is honest, truthful, and sincere in her relationships with adults and children.

Your child's future depends on the quality of health your child enjoys. Good health is essential so your child can turn into a clear-thinking adult. There are several excellent books at your public library on nutrition. Health offices have free materials, and county extension agents have free pamphlets. Your family doctor should certainly be the first person to visit.

An excellent book to read is *Parents' Guide to Nutrition* (Addison-Wesley) by Susan Baker. This book covers everything from acne to yogurt and is very practical and easy to understand.

As Winston Churchill once said, "Had I known I would live so long, I would have taken better care of myself."

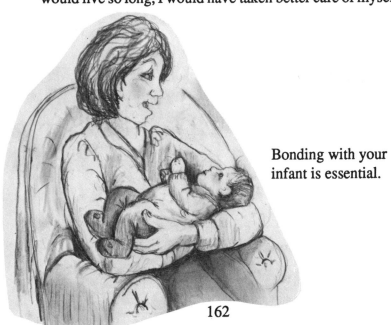

Bonding with your infant is essential.

Chapter Nine

HOME IS YOUR CHILD'S GREATEST INFLUENCE

Your good parenting makes everything else possible.

The home is the single greatest influence on children. Several studies and experiences tell us that the greatest influence on a child is the family. A child's basic personality and values are well-developed before he goes to school. The parents must ask themselves some questions. What kind of influence am I? In the next several years, will my children think about the positive influence that I had upon them, or will they remember the negative thoughts?

As parents, there are several ways you can have a positive influence on your children:

★ Make some time every day to spend privately with each child and use your listening skills to find out what your child is thinking about.

★ Have family rules that are understood by all and be sure to enforce them.

★ Be sure you are fair. Be firm and always apply consequences for unacceptable behavior. One of the greatest compliments a parent can receive from a child is "you are fair."

★ Provide good nutrition, especially a good breakfast, and encourage good health habits. Your example will speak louder than words.

★ Give your child an opportunity to grow creatively by encouraging him to pursue interests.

★ Help your children develop good values and talk about family traditions and beliefs. You are your child's greatest influence. Make great effort to make it a good one.

MOMS ARE INCREDIBLE

Can you remember your children shouting, "Mom!" To an unhurried mom, that can be a precious sound. Your child probably didn't need much. Maybe he wanted the assurance that you were close by or maybe a chance to talk about his favorite toy or what he was going to do when Grandpa and Grandma came to visit.

Linda Weber, in her book *Mom, You're Incredible*, says "I wouldn't trade anything for our time together; the unhurried seasons when I didn't have to worry about fitting my mothering into a crowded schedule."

Studies by child psychologists suggest that babies failing to bond with their mothers during their first two years developed behavior problems later in life. Children never stop needing your unhurried nurturing

No investment you make in life will yield the returns you'll get from nurturing your children. Enjoy your role of protecting, feeding, encouraging, strengthening, bonding, and establishing your kids.

A GOOD FATHER IS ALSO A GOOD TEACHER

While traveling a few years back, I saw a large billboard that read, "There are two things that keep kids off drugs: a mother and a father." That has been true in the past and is more true today. A practicing psychiatrist who works with recovering drug addicts said, "Children with fathers who are involved with their kids are more apt not to get on drugs and stay off."

A good father is a teacher. If he is a teacher, then he does not have to be a disciplinarian. There is a lot of misunderstanding about discipline and punishment. Discipline is teaching a child to behave in ways that the parents consider to be desirable and to avoid behavior considered undesirable. It is a learning process for the child.

Here are four practical pointers that will help all fathers, grandfathers, uncles, and stepfathers:

❖ Develop an understanding of the stages of your children's development from birth through the teens. You need to know what children are capable of doing and what they are not capable of doing at each stage in their development. If you have any experience, you will know what a child can and cannot do. If you don't know, then find out from people who know. The first person to talk with is the child's mother. She is traditionally with the child more and has learned a great deal through observation and some trial and error. You may also ask a good teacher or doctor or read some practical books in your library.

❖ If you want to teach your children desirable behavior, you must develop a positive relationship with them. If your children do not like you, then you are not going to be a good teacher. It really does not take much effort to maintain a good relationship with your children. You must nurture, love, trust and respect. This kind of relationship develops emotional bonding that will last a lifetime. Understand, though, that this deep emotional relationship has to be built in the early years. Be sure to spend one-on-one time with your children every day. This takes a lot of your time, but your children really need and want you.

✧ Be firm with your children, so they will know you mean what you say and will back it up with appropriate consequences. You need to develop a balance between being permissive and being strict. Permissiveness or strictness should only refer to your children's actions, never to your child's feeling. Take time to listen and set boundaries according to the child's development.

✧ Learn how to praise your children for good behavior; for example, "I'm proud of you for taking out the garbage without being told a second time! or "I'm glad you got your homework completed this time." A pat on the back goes a long way. Of course, your good modeling is the very best teacher. If they see you conduct yourself in an undesirable manner, then there is no way you can teach your children desirable behavior. If they admire you, love you, and respect your authority, then you have a good chance of raising children you can be proud of.

There seems to be a direct relationship between the time a father spends with his children and their behavior and academic progress in school.

Here are some other ideas for making a difference in your kids' lives:

✧ Show affection toward your children from infancy through adulthood. Hugs will not make sissies out of boys.

✧ Play with your children.

✧ Read newspapers, magazines, and books to demonstrate

that you value reading and find it both necessary and enjoyable.

✧ When planning a family vacation, obtain maps and brochures that describe the history, geology, and climate of the area you will be visiting. Share the information with your family.

✧ Take your entire family to concerts, museums, and other educational places.

✧ Be sure that every member of the family is at the table for dinner.

✧ Advise your children on the courses they take in high school and suggest they become involved in sports, so they will learn the dynamics of competition and teamwork.

HELP CHILDREN BE SUCCESSFUL

Many parents are interested and concerned that their children succeed as students. Experience tells us that success and achievement start in the home. There's an old rule that says, "Never do for a child what he can do for himself."

If you want your children to become responsible students and adults, you simply let them try, and experience success as well as failure. If they happen to fail, simply say, "I'm glad you tried," or "I'm proud of you for trying so hard." Avoid criticism or ridicule, as it rarely works.

If children can experience success and achievement at home, then they will experience success and are more apt to achieve academically at school.

The key is PATIENCE. You need enough patience to watch, wait, and listen. Let your child try a new task and fail. Then let her make the necessary corrections. All of us learn new tasks by trial and error. Children are not afraid to make errors. What they are afraid of is the ridicule that may come from adults, like "stupid," "dumb," and "your brother or sister can do better."

If your child ever says "I can't," then help that child complete tasks he can do. As a child, I was told many times, "Can't will never do anything." A child should always be encouraged to try. All of us need support from each other from birth through our school years, and on to successful, responsible adulthood. Parents can provide children with the opportunity to accept responsibility and achieve success in the family unit. The following are only a few ideas for areas of responsibility that have worked for many families:

★ Have children pick up toys, books, and other personal items and see that it is done. Accept no excuse for the task that is not done.
★ As early as possible, let children dress themselves.
★ Have children make their own beds and put away clothes. Parents need to be good models.
★ Let children help clean the home—vacuum, dust the furniture, etc.
★ Let children help with the laundry, folding the clothes and putting them away.
★ Have children help with meals when appropriate.
★ Have children clear the table after meals and wash the dishes.
★ If appropriate, encourage children to do some of the shopping.

Children as young as 18 months can take on responsibility by picking up their own toys.

The more responsible children are, the better students they will be at school, because they have experienced the good feelings of success and achievement. Children lacking the experiences of success and achievement become dependent and lack the self-confidence to achieve success as adults.

Occasionally, we see 25-year-old adults who are still dependent on their parents. When children have self-respect, they will in turn respect their parents.

If a child lives with encouragement, he learns confidence!

DO-ABLE TASKS TO ENRICH RELATIONSHIPS

Do-able tasks involve the parent and child doing things together, which the child already knows and needs to practice in order to maintain. The result is a pleasant, helpful homework time for your child.

Some do-able homework can be:

1. Reading to your child
2. Listening to your child read
3. Listening to your child tell a story
4. Telling a child a story
5. Playing table games
6. Doing puzzles

Each of these activities causes the child to use thinking, listening, and other language skills vital for classroom learning.

When does homework help?

❧ When the child and parent have a positive attitude.
❧ When the time is right.
❧ When the task is a "do-able" one that can be enjoyed by both the parent and child
❧ When the task helps the child either to practice what she already knows or to learn a new, exciting skill.

Here are some do-able tasks:

🔥 Make up a problem and see if your child can work out the answer. Example: If we have 12 rolls, then we eat four, how many will be left?

🔥 Let your child make up similar problems and ask you to solve it.

🔥 Using a picture cut from a newspaper or magazine, ask your child to make up a story.

These are just a few examples of how much learning can be reinforced in the home.

You are your child's first and most important teacher. Always keep in touch with your child's teacher and find out what skill is being taught at school, so you can reinforce it at home. The quality time you spend with your children makes a difference in their progress at school.

HELPING YOUR CHILD TASTE SUCCESS

Frequently, children are unsuccessful academically only because they have come to believe they are not capable of doing their assignments, maybe even because of past experiences. These activities will help your child begin to get the good feeling of success:

✗ First day. Take five minutes and have your child tell you his successes. You should share some of your own successes. You do the writing. Don't judge any of the successes, or you will not get any listed. Try putting the successes on time lines, one for you and one for the child.

✗ Second day. Help your child name someone who has helped bring about success for your child. Example: "Mom, you helped me learn to ride my bike," or "Dad taught me to

170

play ball."

✗ <u>Third day</u>. Take five minutes and have your child list his most important successful accomplishments. You should also list your own and share them.

✗ <u>Fourth day</u>. Have your child list the accomplishments he is most proud of. Avoid making comments or judging, then ask these questions: a) What adult would you like to be like when you grow up? b) If you could spend the rest of the year working on a goal, what would it be? Accept any response. Don't argue or make judgmental statements; c) List three words you like for your friends to use to describe you. (For each of these questions, you may want to apply the question to yourself first and share your answer.)

✗ <u>Fifth day</u>. Take 5 or 10 minutes and tell your child what you think he is good at. Encourage your child to tell you what you're good at. You'll be pleasantly surprised with the results. You might say, "You're good at putting your clothes away." Then the child might respond, "Mom, I like your cookies." You should write down the responses, then exchange the list after each of you have written five or six things. Be honest.

✗ <u>Sixth day</u>. Learn to give your children appropriate praise for the little things they do successfully. Find your children doing something good and let them know they are good at it.

These activities will take only 5 - 10 minutes, and they are very important for your child's future success. Remember, big successes can come only after little successes. Help your children discover that they can be successful.

FINDING PERSONAL STRENGTHS

So many kids live in a negative environment. It is hard

for them to see the good in their personal lives, when they are bombarded with negative statements. Families need to learn to pat each other on the back and help each other find personal strengths.

I know a family of four with two foster children who spend time each Friday talking about each family member. They can say only good things, like "Dad, I like your mustache. It tickles me when you kiss me goodnight."

Here are some ideas that will help your family develop personal strengths:

℗ During a quiet time or at dinner with the entire family, say something about each family member's personal strength; for example, "Jimmy, I like your good sense of humor."

℗ At another family gathering, each family member should tell what his personal strengths are. Avoid making wise cracks or ridiculing. Example: "I'm good in math, and I think I'll be an engineer," or "I enjoy this family when we share with each other."

℗ During another family gathering have members discuss a personal strength they wish they had. Example: "I'd like to be taller," or "I wish I was better in math. It would make my job easier." This gives the other family members an opportunity to be supportive.

℗ Ask each family member to tell what it is that is keeping them from using the strength they want to have.

The power of helping individual family members develop personal strengths is tremendous and long-lasting.

TAKING THE PRESSURE OFF PLAY

The pressure to engage in organized, competitive sports and camps is one of the most obvious pressures on

172

contemporary children to grow up too fast. Sports camps, especially, are dedicated to developing the finer points of athletics and competition. They are frequently under the direction of professional athletes. The daily routine is rigorous, with individual and group lessons, practice sessions, and tournaments complete with trophies.

These summer programs demonstrate the new attitudes that the years of childhood are not to be frittered away by engaging in mere fun. Childhood years must be put to use perfecting skills and abilities. Children are initiated early into the rigors of adult competition.

The pressures to grow up quickly, to achieve early in the arenas of sports, academics, and social interaction is great in middle-class America. There is no room today for "late bloomers." Children have to achieve success early or be regarded as losers.

We can't change our hurried society, but there are some things we can do to take the pressure off our children.

❀ Being polite to children is very important and will do much to improve parent-child relations.

❀ For school-age children, it is important to communicate your appreciation for all the good things they do for you, like helping around the house or baby-sitting younger siblings. You must remember that they are still children, and some things they don't need to be burdened with.

❀ Pressured children tend to blame their parents for the pressures they have. Frequently, the parents are overscheduled and hurrying themselves. Parents must first take the pressures off themselves, so they can have time to talk and listen to their children.

❀ Avoid pressure to participate in competitive athletics. Once I asked a 16-year-old why he doesn't like athletics in high school. He answered, "I had to play little league." Parents need to let kids make their own decisions about whether to participate in competitive sports. When children do decide to play in a sport, parents need to relax and let the child enjoy playing. Don't worry about winning and losing.

❀ Parents need to take the pressure out of play. Kids need to play on their own terms. I do not believe elementary age children are emotionally and physically mature enough to take part in the rigors of competitive sports. Kids do like to compete, but on their own terms, not those of adults. I know a school where the third through eighth graders play softball. They choose up teams and everyone gets to play. They don't even keep score. When asked how they know who wins, their answer is, "We're just playing for fun." Now that's the way play should be.

Play for children should be looked upon as preparation for life. Just as kitten's play is preparing it to survive in the real world, childhood does not mean it is always a happy, innocent period. Rather, it is an important period in life to which all children are entitled.

DON'T PRESSURE YOUR CHILD TO BE THE BEST

Dr. James Dobson, in his book *Dare to Discipline*, says, "All parents pray that their baby will be normal at birth, then after they are born, they want them to be gifted."

Problems can arise when parents insist that their children get top grades in school. Undue pressure can cause stress, which can eventually lead to illness. An elementary school principal told me there were several children in his school with ulcers. Children under pressure to excel may eventually give up. They may develop an "it's not worth it" attitude. They may rebel and become behavior problems. Or they may keep the pressure inside themselves and begin to dislike school.

If you think your child is bright or gifted, but not achieving up to his ability, back off a little and learn how to enrich your child's life.

❀ Take your children to museums and art galleries.
❀ Go on field trips that they are interested in. Find out what the class is studying, then plan a trip that will enrich the school lesson.
❀ Take a trip through books. Books can take a child anywhere, to anything, satisfying a curiosity or a fantasy.
❀ Introduce your child to computers. (Get sound advice before you invest the money in computers, though.)
❀ Take time to read to your children, especially the classics.
❀ Take your child to lectures and film presentations in the community, then get books and talk about the lecture.
❀ Take your child to concerts.

Many teachers have asked, "What's wrong with being average academically?" Why can't we back off and let children be children and enjoy their childhood? Studies tell us that happy children become happy, productive adults. Most of the work done in this world is by average people, like you and me.

Some very wise person once said, "Childhood is a journey—not a race to be the best."

KIDS LEARN FROM THEIR MISTAKES

Children who excel in academics love school. Those who have a difficult time take pride in being different and having interests outside of school. As parents, you need to honor those nonacademic interests that your children may have. Every time your child cannot grasp what others find easy, help your child concentrate on something he is good at—

175

be it drawing, socializing, sports, etc.

Everyone needs to find what they are good at. It is a healthy attitude and one that will ensure survival in the world. Children have a way of ignoring what is uncomfortable for them. It doesn't really matter how much or how often they are scolded for "not doing your best" or for making a mistake.

I am not a good speller, but that does not mean I can't write. When I teach a class, I tell them that I'm the world's worst speller. Then they tell me what they are good or bad at. The need to look good runs too deeply in our society. There is always the fear that, if you point out the mistakes and failures you feel within yourself, you will lose respect, love, and friendship.

As parents, you want your children to do their best, to succeed. It is hard to accept the red marks that come home on your child's papers. It is hard to believe that it may not be within your child, but rather in your own need for perfection.

Keep in mind that mistakes are not a sign of failure. Mistakes should be a means of growth. Your scolding, lecturing, and helping to correct each mistake you see will not help. Let your child know that less-than-perfect papers are accepted by you. Try to use imperfections as a tool to good, positive communication.

Mistakes are a sign of not understanding. Let your child know that you can discuss the problem together. If mistakes are foolish and show a lack of caring, forcing your child to do it over to prove that he can do better will destroy enthusiasm for learning and build resentment for school.

These activities will help your child improve the quality of school work:

- Set goals for working toward excellence. Provide activities that build an inner sense of accomplishment. Avoid using money, promises, or gifts.

176

- Encourage your child to share stories and essays with the family. Ask her to share or read favorite selections of a story with you. Have your child make up a math problem that will stump the family. Have your child get involved in the family finances by working out a family budget that is fair to everyone.
- Encourage your child to enter local art and writing contests. Include your children in your discussions of community and world affairs.
- Let your child know that mistakes are nothing to be ashamed of. They do not affect your love and respect for your children.
- Tell your child about your own mistakes. Admit them and learn to laugh at them. We all need to take ourselves a little less seriously.
- Try changing uncomfortable aspects of your personality, habits, and parenting practices. Discuss with your child why you want to make some changes and the help you need in trying to make the changes. Be open and honest.

Let your child know that perfection is a dream, not a goal. Mistakes seem to be necessary and very human. Our ability to laugh at our sometimes dumb mistakes are to help us learn and to improve ourselves.

HELPING YOUR CHILDREN BE POSITIVE

If you want your kids to be happy and well-adjusted, it must begin with you. Happiness is contagious. It is hard to teach happiness. It has become a part of our culture to make sarcastic remarks to other people, to put them down, to complain about everyone and everything. When we fall into the complaining habit, it affects our whole attitude about others and about life in general. We begin to feel that things are bad and unfair and that we deserve something better.

People who were once positive and uplifting can become frustrated and depressed just because the trend of negative attitudes has taken hold of their lives. Negative attitudes can be contagious, too.

Are you creating a happy family life and minimizing the bad things that happen? We all hear about the bad things that are happening. It would be easy to get discouraged about the bad news we hear and read daily, but what good would that do? You need to count the good things, your blessings. Try to focus on the good. Then, when your kids do the same, reinforce it.

In your home, do you thank your kids for saying "thank you"? That is positive reinforcement. If will have lasting effects on your kids' future behavior. You need to help your kids by example to find positive things to say. It needs to become a rule and then a habit. At mealtime, do you enjoy each other, or is mealtime a gripe and complain time? Find more positive things to say about activities and people. Have you ever heard the expression, "Accentuate the positive; eliminate the negative"?

When your kids start complaining about school, their friends, athletics, and negative things in general, try saying, "Oh, be thankful for the good things you've got." The song instructs your kids and tells them why and what their response should be. Your kids should hear from you that you don't want to hear complaining. They need to hear you saying positive things about them and their behavior. Teach your children to be thankful for the good things in their lives.

Give attention to spotting the negative thinking in your home and lead by your example away from the negative and toward the positive.

Be thankful, rather than griping.
Be self-confident, rather than the doubter.
Be peaceful, rather than arguing.
Be trusting, rather than suspicious.
Be certain, rather than apprehensive.
Be rested, rather than restless.
Be secure, rather than fearful.
Be free, rather than in bondage.

Note: Copy this on a poster or have it enlarged and put it on your bulletin board.

If you create an environment that is motivational when your children are home, it will get them through college and much more.

Your children will grow up to be like you, whether they want to or not. Children live out what they've seen lived within your home. What are you modeling for your children? You need to be that quiet, steady, supportive influence who calms the storms and makes the children feel important. It takes time and dedication, but it is worth every bit of it.

IS YOUR FAMILY MATERIALISTIC?

In Dolores Curran's book, *Traits of a Healthy Family*, she reported in her study of families that those who support a cause and are active members of their church are not as materialist or pleasure-seeking as other families.

Families who do not have a purpose will buy things to alleviate that innate hunger for a purpose. If things aren't going well in a family and the parents wonder why they work so hard with little or no gratification, they can always buy a car. Or they can buy a more expensive home or new furniture.

One lady explained, "We're not getting along, so we decided to buy a motor home." If the family is not getting along, how will a motor home help? Families are actually looking for close relationships with each other. What they were really seeking was a way to enjoy the beautiful outdoor environment together. That is what most families are really wanting, not a new motorhome to show off.

FIGHTING BACK AGAINST TV VIOLENCE

Violence in America has become a national concern. Studies do show that the more violence your kids see on TV the more they regard violence as a normal way to resolve problems. When your kids watch violence, they lose the ability to empathize with others and become suspicious and less likely to help victims of real violence. Kids begin to feel insecure.

Many children are watching 1,000 rapes, homicides, or assaults on TV every year. The research indicates that the more violence kids see on TV the more aggressive they become.

Before 1970, parents, teachers, friends, and peers influenced children, in that order. Now, parents and teachers have lost their influence on children. The greatest influences are movies, audio tapes, radio, and computer, in that order. So who is teaching your child values? TV or you?

If you are like most parents, you sense that TV is not all that great for your children. You are right. Research now tells us the facts about TV and your children. Those Saturday morning cartoons are chock full of violence. Eighty percent of what children watch is meant for adults. Children get the idea that this is a mean world and learn from TV that they need to be mean. Children who watch too much TV are more likely to start a fight, to stand by and watch and encourage fighting, rather than walking away.

If given a choice, most kids would rather play team

sports, go to parties, and take care of pets than watch TV. Kids get more satisfaction out of learning a new skill and solving a puzzle.

If you learn to limit and monitor your children's TV viewing, then they will have more time to read, play with friends, do homework, and be creative. They will learn to think and will learn acceptable social behavior from you.

Infants and toddlers are affected by angry faces and loud music. Research tells us that toddlers are affected by angry confrontations and action-adventure programs and can be upset by them. Safer choices are home videos with lots of happy faces and programs with kids' songs. Your public library has good videos that are free. You should watch the program with your very young child so you can talk about it and share it with her. Public TV has the highest quality programs for infants and toddlers.

Children ages 2 to 5 cannot distinguish between fantasy and reality, real and cartoon violence. Appropriate programs for these kids can be found on public television. At this age, they are learning social behavior and cognitive skills. They will pick up a desire for food and toys and antisocial behavior from those Saturday morning cartoons that everyone seems to think are so innocent.

You need to discuss what is real and what is make-believe. Talk about violence on TV. Explain that hitting and punching in real life is not funny or acceptable. Establish limits of two hours of TV per day and no watching after 8 p.m.

School-aged children (5-12) can be influenced by commercials and can be scared by violent events on TV. You should monitor programs and choose those that support your values. Help your child analyze commercials by saying, "What do you think they are trying to sell us now?" Get the TV guide and plan what your child can see weekly. Make sure they don't watch any television until their homework is done.

If you want to do something about violence on TV, voice your concerns by writing to:

ABC, 77 W. 66th St., New York, N.Y. 10023, Attention: Audience Information.

CBS, 555 W. 52, New York, N.Y. 10019, Attention: Programming Department.

NBC, 30 Rockefeller Plaza, New York, N.Y. 10112, Attention: Program Office.

FOX, Lucie Salhany, 3000 W. Alemeda Ave., Burbank, Calif. 91523.

Also write to Reed E. Hundt, Chairman, FCC, 1919 M St., N.W., Washington, D.C. 20554. Tell him that you want networks to have one hour of TV for children every day.

You need to be in control of the TV, or you won't be in charge of your kids.

THE ART OF STORYTELLING

The art of storytelling is a very old one that has survived for many, many centuries.

Storytelling is something that all parents and grandparents can and should do. When can you tell a story? Anytime when you think your child needs to be settled down, when he is recovering from a sickness, at mealtime, and before going to sleep.

Begin by telling a story you are familiar with, like one you may recall from your own childhood. Children love to hear stories about what life was like when you were their age.

Anyone can be a storyteller. My own grandchildren are always saying, "Tell me a story." I ask them what they want to hear about, and they will say, "When you were a boy." Or they will want to know what life was like in the 1930s or

1950s.

Make up a story using ideas you know will interest your child. Just be sure the plot has some form to it by having a beginning, middle, and ending that link together and make sense. Here are some other storytelling ideas:

✎ Tell about things you did when you were a child.
✎ Tell about unusual happenings in your childhood, including incidents with siblings.
✎ Use your imagination to tell tall tales, like "The Adventures of the Fish That Got Away," "The Puppy That Went to School," "The Doll That Started Talking," or "When I Was in the First Grade."
✎ Look at pictures in books and magazines to get ideas. Cut out any that will help illustrate your story.
✎ Make a simple puppet or use toys to dramatize your story. You can try tying a piece of cloth or handkerchief over your hand or finger. Draw a face on it and move it around for a puppet.
✎ If you want to get really involved, try a flannel board with figures and scenery to illustrate stories. Flannel boards can be purchased or you can make your own. *Handbook for Storytellers* by Caroline Feller Bauer includes a chapter on flannel boards and is very helpful for a beginner. It tells you how to tell stories, lists sources of storytelling, plus much more information.

When you tell stories, your children will be eager to tell their own stories. You will want to encourage your child to tell stories. For younger children, try writing down what he tells you. Then you can print or type the stories.

Your storytelling times will develop important listening skills, expressive oral language, and family history and will help children understand who they are.

SUCCESS STARTS EARLY!

Section Five

START EARLY—Building Career Awareness
**Chapter 10: How Children Learn
About Careers
Chapter 11: College & Your Child**

> Establishing a career is something that comes with time. What is important, however, is that your student begins to familiarize himself with options that he finds interesting.
>
> —Shawn Answerson
> from *Countdown to College*

Chapter Ten

HOW CHILDREN LEARN
ABOUT CAREERS

Many parents are concerned about the kind of careers their children will choose. All parents want their children to be successful. However, we can show our prejudice about career preferences by our comments. What happens when we ask children, "What would you like to be when you grow up?" If your daughter replied, "I want to be a mechanic," you might respond with, "That is a job for boys!"

Parents are the closest role models children have to follow. It is not unusual to see children pursuing the same type of career as their parents. Nothing is wrong with that if your children choose their career because of their own interests and not because of mom's or dad's interests.

Here are some ways to help your child prepare for a future career:

☞ Through your own example, your children need to develop a sense of pride about careers, so that whatever they choose to do, whether at home or at school, they will have a sense of worth about themselves and their chosen lifestyle.
☞ Give them chores that will help prepare them for the jobs they will hold later in life and let them know why they are

186

doing those chores.

☞ Explain to your child that the things you and the school stress are important. Being responsible and dependable are life skills that will last a lifetime, and these skills are valued by future employers. Teach your children that being on time for school is just as important as being on time for a job.

☞ Give your child the opportunity of seeing adults who are improving their own job skills by taking courses, reading books, or receiving special training. This will help them understand that education does not end once a person leaves school. It continues throughout life.

☞ As you take family trips, point out some of the occupations that you see represented—the jobs associated with highway construction, a busy airport, a hotel, a restaurant, etc.

☞ Help your children accept that all jobs and careers are good and honorable. If they want to be a butcher, encourage them to be the best butcher they can be.

Skills are not the only factors in being a good employee. Attitude, ability to cooperate, and ability to rationalize contribute greatly to success, both in school and on the job.

The following books can be found at your public library:

How to Help Your Child Plan a Career by Diane Edelman Gersoni gives suggestions on how parents can help children keep an open mind about career choices.

And What Do You Do? by George Ancona describes 21 careers that do not require a college education.

Who Works Here? by Caroline Arnold tells about the many careers within a community.

HELPING WITH CAREER DECISIONS

Your children need the information and encouragement you can provide to make the right career choices. You should:

X Encourage your children to talk with the high school counselor.

X Make sure your college freshman talks to a career counselor at the college she is attending. Every freshman should take a free aptitude test to help identify interests and skills.

X Teachers at high schools and colleges make great mentors. They can gather more information that will give students reassurance about their career decisions.

X Have honest discussions with your children about the fact that their career may change during their lifetime. What they do in their twenties may change when they are in their thirties. In years gone by, a person chose a career and stayed with it all his life. Now, a person may have as many as a dozen different careers in a lifetime. Even in careers such as teaching, medicine, and engineering, professionals must study to keep up with current practices and technology. Students should be encouraged to start up their own businesses when appropriate. They just might find greater security and satisfaction.

X Do not be disappointed if your child's career plans change. In fact, change should be encouraged. New information may cast negative light on the original choice. We are living in a time of rapid change. You need to help your children accept change in order to survive in the job market.

X If your child can't make a decision by the second year of college, insist on a career counselor to help him sort out the options. The student must, of course, make the final decision. Testing is not always the answer, but can be a valuable tool for gathering important information.

X Encourage your child to go into an apprenticeship to get a better idea whether the chosen field is a good fit. Volunteering is another way to find out what a profession is really like. One young lady I know volunteered at the local hospital to see if nursing was right for her. As it turned out, she decided working with sick people was really not what she liked doing.

X Encourage your child to access sources of career information. Colleges now have computer programs to help explore careers. The U.S. Department of Labor's *Dictionary of Occupational Titles* and their *Occupational Outlook Handbook* can both be found at the local library. They are musts for students wanting the latest information on job prospects, requirements, and rewards.

EARLY CAREER AWARENESS

My father always told me, "If you find a job you love, you'll never have to work a day in your life." There are 23,000 job titles. By the time your child joins the work force, there will be many more.

The more information and awareness your child gains, the better the opportunities. Children at a very early age become aware of the work that adults do. They know, for example, that you leave the home and go to a work place. You can start by talking about your job and the jobs your friends have. By five years of age, children should know that people work and have careers.

These activities can help your elementary-age child develop a better awareness of careers:

X For 3 to 5 minutes, list on a piece of paper the different jobs and careers your friends, relatives and neighbors have.

X Help your child create a family tree of occupations, listing the careers of grandparents, uncles, aunts, and older siblings. On posterboard, draw a large tree. Cut 2" to 5" strips of paper, and write a career on each. Attach to the tree.

(Ages 9 and up):

✳ Encourage your child to start a career book. Let him choose occupations that seem interesting. For each occupation, your child should determine the skills needed, a description of the workplace, and the education required.

✳ Take a job walk. As you and your child walk a block or two around your neighborhood, have him notice people working in particular occupations. Look for situations that will require a worker to repair something, such as a bent fender on a car or a pothole in the street. When you return home, help your child record the findings on a large sheet of paper. Then post it on the wall.

✳ Play a version of 20 questions based on different types of occupations. Players think of a job and describe it. The opponents try to guess the job. The team that scores the most correct guesses with the fewest questions wins.

✳ On a piece of paper, list the following categories:

Working with hands	Working outdoors
Working at a desk	Working with people
Working alone	Driving a vehicle
Giving directions	Working with tools
Traveling	Working with money

Using the occupation word list, put each occupation under the appropriate job category.

Using the occupation word list, divide the jobs into the categories, "Hard Work," "Fun Work," and "Both." (Ages 3-8)

✳ Get a can of food and brainstorm all the jobs that are necessary to get that can of food into your home for your use. Example: farmer, soil scientist, extension agent, cannery worker, truck driver, stock person, cashier.

✳ Before reading a book to your child, discuss all the people it took to get this book into your hands. Example: author, publisher, editors, artists, tree feller, paper factory worker.

✳ Make arrangements to take your child to a factory or plant that produces a product and let your child see all the various jobs required to produce that item.

✳ After watching a TV program together, list all the careers required to put the program together. Example: writer, producer, director, make-up artist, lighting technician, camera operators, etc.

✳ Let your child cut out pictures of people working from newspapers and magazines, then paste them on a large sheet of paper (18" x 24"). (Ages 5-8)

✳ Ask grandparents to look at the word list with you and tell which of these occupations did not exist when they were children. (Ages 7-12)

DEVELOPING WORK ETHICS

Encourage your children to participate in household tasks to the best of their ability. Watching your child at play will help you to select work he can manage. These do-able tasks are things children ages 2 to 5 can do in the kitchen. All of these jobs require close adult supervision.

Tear lettuce for salad
Snap green beans
Shell fresh peas
Mash potatoes
Stir pancake batter
Scramble eggs
Put bread in toaster

Mix orange juice
Add ingredients to cookie dough
Set the table
Help with grocery shopping

Here are some social tasks for 2- to 5-year-olds:

Answer the telephone
Tell a story to the family (one sentence might
be enough)
Get the mail
Serve a snack
Round up the family at mealtime
Plan a birthday party
Share in rule-making
Decide which clothes to wear or buy

Ages 6 to 12: Children in this age group can perform all the jobs that younger children are learning, but they can do them better and stay on task longer. They tend to be self-critical about the quality of their work. They are generally cooperative.

Cook and clean up
Wash windows
Clean car
Bake cookies
Babysit a younger sibling
Tutor a younger child
Help with your business
Load a dishwasher and turn it on
Use washing machine and dryer
Use a microwave
Feed and care for family pets

Grow a vegetable and flower garden (try selling some)
Sew on missing buttons
Take out garbage
Mow and water the lawn
Shop for groceries
Help paint

These tasks develop social skills for 6- to 12-year-olds:

Answer the phone and take messages
Write thank-you notes
Join a club
Invite friends over
Sleep over at a friend's house
Run errands for you and a neighbor
Do odd jobs for others
Participate in family discussions
Plan a party
Remember relatives' birthdays and anniversaries
Select and purchase clothes with parental approval
Volunteer for school and community projects

To teach loyalty and love, let your child have a pet. Nearly all executives say that they had a pet dog or cat as a child. A pet will help your child develop traits that employers want: love, devotion, cooperation, loyalty, and sacrifice. If your child gets a pet, be sure that the care and well-being of the pet is the child's responsibility.

Teenagers have learned to organize their lives, with activities like homework, school, chores, after-school jobs, social involvement with friends, and school and community activities. During these teen years, there is a dramatic shift toward wanting independence. Parents have an awesome responsibility to respond with different problems and solutions. Remember, you have just a few years to help your teenager learn to be self-reliant, self-motivated, responsible, and dependable, so she will be successful at college and in the workplace.

If your teenagers get a paid job outside the home after school and on weekends, make sure they do not overextend themselves, or their grades will suffer. Most parents of successful students limit their teenager to 10 to 15 hours of work for pay per week. Summer jobs are an excellent way to learn about what work for pay is really all about, and teens can find out what they do not like to do.

TELLING YOUR CHILDREN ABOUT YOUR CAREER

Children need to know what you do. My grandchildren love to hear stories about what work was like when I was a boy their age. They also want to hear what life was like with my parents and grandparents. They need to know what people earned 50 years ago, or even 25 years ago. One cattle rancher told me that it took just as many cows to buy a car in 1936 as it does in 1996. These are the kinds of things kids need to know.

Children have a need to hear about jobs of the past. They want to know your work history during their elementary school years. They also want to know what you do between morning and night.

I know a father who took his daughter out to take care of their cows when they were calving. She followed him around wherever he went. She helped her dad do a cesarean on a cow that was having trouble giving birth to her first calf.

194

Today, that daughter is finishing her studies in veterinary medicine. Parents make a mistake by insisting that their children follow in their footsteps.

When you show your children what you do and discuss your work, your children will not be one of the 300 children who were not able to answer the questions "What do your parents do?" Over 91% of elementary students could not tell their teacher what their parents do.

CAREER COUNSELING FOR YOUR CHILD

Most high schools have a career counseling office that is available to parents and students. Schools now offer career awareness courses that help students identify their strengths. Don't get too excited, however, if your child is not set on a career in high school. Students should leave their options open, and by the junior year of college, they should know what career they want to pursue.

An apprenticeship in some job just might be the right thing for some young people. I knew a young man who graduated from high school and had already earned his journeyman as a butcher. He worked for a locally owned supermarket as an apprentice. Upon graduating, he started out at $12/hour. That adds up to $23,000—plus benefits. There would be opportunities for advancements in a large grocery chain and the possibilities of going to a community college and taking courses in business.

For some young people, to earn before learning is the only way to find out the real value of a college education. Education is the key to higher income. These figures are based on 1993 average income:

1. Less than 9th-grade education: $13,000/year
2. 9th grade to 12th grade: $17,000/year

195

3. High school graduate:	$23,000/year
4. Some college; no degree:	$27,000/year
5. Bachelor's degree:	$36,000/year
6. Master's degree:	$46,000/year
7. Professional degree:	$75,000+/yr
8. Doctoral degree:	$60,000+/yr

Many jobs without a degree can be a dead end. There are few advancements without a degree.

Not every high school graduate should go to college. What about the child who wants to take a break after high school and get a job? A little time out may be just what your child needs. Some parents may panic, fearing their child will never go to college. The majority of young people who decide to work a year or two before college usually do end up going. Many college teachers report that college students who don't want to be in college are usually not successful students. They are not motivated. They may be there only because their parents wanted them to go.

CAREERS IN THE YEAR 2000 AND BEYOND

Because of technology, there are new fields emerging every year and making some jobs obsolete. There will be more discoveries which will bring about greater opportunities and completely new careers.

Once a source of reliable employment, jobs in fields such as lumber, automobiles, mining, agriculture, ship building, medicine, and law are highly competitive. Climbing the corporate ladder is risky, because of company mergers, streamlining, and downsizing the corporate management.

Every time there is a loss of jobs in one industry, there is a gain in another field. An example is the agricultural industry. Machines that can do the work of many employees caused job loss. I can recall the 1950s, when cotton pickers were in great demand because cotton had to be picked by hand. Now, universal education through high school has become a reality. Today, there are more people teaching than there are people working at farm jobs. Teaching jobs pay more than farm jobs, and they are more satisfying.

The following careers will be emerging:

○ Robots will do the work that many factory workers were doing in years gone by. Keeping these robots working will provide more specialized and better-paying jobs than the jobs the robots replaced. Some predict that robot engineering will be the best paying job in the year 2000.

○ Computers are here to stay. It is estimated that nearly 85 percent of American homes have a computer. At the beginning of the nineties, very few homes had computers. In just six short years, computers have become practically as common as toasters. There is a need to keep the computers running. As new generations are developed, businesses and families will want the latest in computers. Computer programmers will be needed. Books as we know it may become obsolete. Computer manufacturers dream of having a computer in every home, just as the auto industry wanted a car in every garage.

○ Bionics are now a reality. If you need a new hip, leg, arm, foot, hand, or heart, it will be available. This is a field that will be very specialized. There will be a great need for technicians, doctors, scientists, manufacturers, and a new field of psychiatrists emerging.

○ Lasers have been around for a long time. In medicine, there are new uses for lasers. As new uses are discovered, there will be a great need for workers with many different skills, such as chemists, engineers, scientists, and technicians.

○ Energy will always be needed. As the planet runs out of

fossil fuel, new developments will emerge. As synthetic fuels are developed, job opportunities for engineers and technicians will increase.

◎ Managing waste will become a whole new area of career possibilities, as we become more aware of the health problems related to radiological, biological, and chemical residue polluting our water and air. There is a need for research and a work force to correct some of the areas that have been neglected by past practices.

◎ Biological engineering is an emerging field—designing new plants and improving animal growth. There is a need to develop disease-resistant plant life. We need to learn now to convert waste into cheap fuel. There will be professional jobs in fields of biology that are unknown at this time.

◎ Space technology will emerge as a new way to travel. Space laboratories will be developed. You will be able to travel to Europe by space lines, as easy as going to a city in a neighboring state. Space colonies might even be developed. Within the next two decades, astronomy will be a field in which young star-gazers of today will earn a living.

◎ Marine biologists will be studying new ways to harvest the great riches of the ocean. There is little demand for oceanographers now, but there will be emerging professions for the creative young mind.

◎ The food service sector will boom in the future. More food will be prepackaged, and meals will be easier to prepare. Colleges offering courses in restaurant and hotel management place 100 percent of their graduates. As new breeds of restaurants spring up, the head chefs will earn $150,000—an owner-chef of a restaurant, over $1/2 million a year. If your child likes to mess around in the kitchen now, you might have a future millionaire.

◎ Elder care is a field that is growing. In the early part of the

1900s, life expectancy was 40. Now the average American can expect to live to 80 with a good quality life. By the year 2000, nearly 20 percent of the U.S. population will become middle-aged. Those were the babies born after World War II, referred to as the baby boomers. By the year 2020, they'll be in their 70s. Jobs in plastic surgery, recreation, health care, education, and nutrition will zoom. Colleges will be offering majors in geriatrics. There will be specially trained workers in the areas of mental health, physical fitness, and dentistry who will make house calls. There will be a need for retirement consultants. Age 65 is no longer relevant. People are and will be able to live longer and better. Our society needs to rethink the idea of putting our wisest people out to pasture before their time. Consultants will be hired to determine whether an individual is too old to work. Those who retire will need counseling on how and where to spend their retirement years.

PLANNING A CAREER FOR THE YEAR 2000 AND BEYOND

In years gone by, people did not do much planning for their careers. Many people took any job they could get. Until the eighties, there were not many opportunities for daughters. Some hopped from one job to another.

These 10 questions will help your child decide for now what she wants to do:

1. Are there opportunities for the work I'm planning? ___Yes ___No
2. Why am I attracted to this kind of work?
3. How much college does it require? ___years

4. How long is the apprenticeship?_____ years
5. Should I volunteer or get a summer job? ___ Yes___ No
6. Will I be satisfied with the pay?

   Pay range: $_____
7. What are the opportunities for advancement?

_____

8. What do I have to do to get a promotion?

_____

9. What part of the country have the best
opportunities?_____
10. Can I be self-employed? ___ Yes   ___ No
11. Will my chosen career become obsolete?
___ Yes   ___ No
12. Will the career take me away from home for long periods
of time? ___ Yes ___No

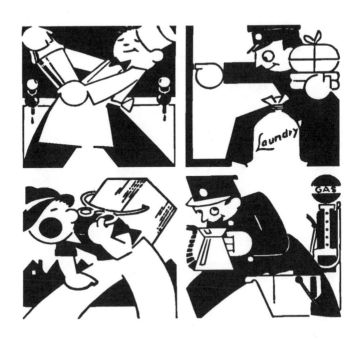

Chapter Eleven

HOW TO GET YOUR CHILD
INTO THE RIGHT COLLEGE

So, you want your child to go to college? That's right—many parents want their children to go to college or some kind of post high school training. There are some simple, easy things any parent can do, and here are some:

✔ When your child is about eight-years-old, begin talking about when he goes to college. Your child needs to know that college education is expected, just as starting kindergarten and then to the first grade, learning to read is expected. At mealtime, college should be discussed.

✔ Expect your children to do their best every day at school when they first go to kindergarten. Make room for some mistakes and avoid perfection. Getting all A's is not your goal. Let those mistakes be a learning experience.

✔ Let your children know that learning is a lifelong experience. Take time to talk about how you are learning on your job and how your job is changing with new technology.

✔ Plan trips to museums, go to concerts with your kids at an early age so they will become accustomed to going with you. Visit book stores and let your children purchase books when appropriate.

✓ Plan vacations that will help your children expand their knowledge. Visit national parks and listen to the fireside talks.

✓ Read to your children daily and let them see you enjoying reading. Then they will learn to value reading as a lifelong learning activity.

✓ Make sure your children are successful students at school. If a child is having problems at school, make an appointment with your child's teacher and find out what the problem is. Make sure your comments are positive about your child's teacher and school. If appropriate, the child should be present at part of the conference.

✓ By the third grade, discuss the fact that you are working and saving money so your child will be able to go to college. When your child is old enough to earn money, open a savings account and encourage your child to put some of the money earned in the bank for college.

✓ For Christmas and birthdays, give your children savings bonds to be used for their college education. Or invest some money in secure bonds that will earn money.

✓ Children who have gone to college had parents who were very supportive in their comments about school, and who supported their school activities.

✓ During high school, limit the number of times per week they can go out with friends. Make sure they are at home on school nights. Be sure you know where they are going, what activity they are going to and set a time when they will be home. Have consequences for not complying with agreed-upon rules.

✓ When your child gets old enough to work, limit the hours to 15 hours each week so he will have time for homework and school activities. Parents I've talked to limit the activities children can take part in. High school students, like some adults, get involved in many activities, and their grades suffer.

Remember, being a parent takes time, energy, love, compassion and some skills on how to treat another human being. Yes, you'll make some mistakes, but if you keep your cool and use some good judgment, you'll be successful in getting your children to college. If you do your part, then they will meet the challenge. It will be worth the effort.

SCHOOLS IN THE YEAR 2000 AND BEYOND

Students' admission to college will be judged by what they can do, rather than their grade point average. Students will be asked to analyze art or a musical performance. They will be required to use a second language, show understanding of geometry or trigonometry and explain certain social issues. They will be asked to respond to community service activities.

For example, in the year 2001 Oregon's public colleges and universities will have new admission standards— the Proficiency-based Admission Standards System (PASS). College freshmen will be required to prove proficiency in six subject areas: mathematics, science, social studies, second language, literature, visual arts, and performing arts.

Students going to college will be required to learn subject matter in their primary and secondary school years. They will begin to take more challenging courses, such as chemistry and physics and a foreign language. They will not have to worry about their GPA. They will need to include samples of their high school work. They will begin to keep a file of their work to demonstrate that they can do it.

The new standards will requie student to demonstrate that they can use the content knowledge they have accumulated. High schools and colleges will truly be able to raise standards. The new standards will only admit students who are prepared for college courses. Colleges will admit students with the confidence that they can do the work. In the future, high schools will not be bound by course units. Students will not have to earn a certain number of credits to graduate from high school.

If your child is struggling in a particular subject area, do what one wise parent did. She hired a tutor to help her son in math. He hated school, simply because of two areas in which he was deficient: math and handwriting. He could read at the tenth-grade level when he was in the fourth grade.

The boy worked with a tutor after school every Monday through Thursday. After a month, I asked him how school was going. "It's great," he said. "I understand long division now."

I looked at his spelling paper and commented, "You only misspelled two words out of 20." His answer was: "My teacher can read my writing now." Before, it was always bad teachers who were the problem. Now that he can do better, the teachers have gotten better.

Start early getting your children ready for college by being sure they are able to "do." If not, then get help if you, yourself, can't help. Not all parents can afford a tutor after school. If you'll just work with your child's teacher, things will improve. If your child knows that you and the teacher are working together, things will get better.

SCHOLARSHIPS AND FINANCIAL ASSISTANCE

If your child needs financial aid, start early in high school and get acquainted with what is available. Education after high school is expensive, and you need to talk to your high school careers counselor, so you can be informed about what is available. Sources you can use to find out about student financial aid include the following:

✧ Contact the financial aide administrator at the college where your child wants to attend.

✧ Contact the higher education agency in your state to find out what is available. Each state has a State Student Incentive Grant (SSIG) program. These programs are jointly funded by your state and the US Department of Education.

✧ If your child has good grades, then you'll want to check out the Robert C. Byrd Honor Scholarship program. Your child must demonstrate outstanding academic achievement and show promise of success as a college student. You can call 1-800-433-3243 for information.

✧ You will want to investigate the AmeriCorps program that provides full-time educational awards in return for community service. The program is flexible, in that the student can work before, during, and after attending college. Call 1-800-942-2677 or write to The Corporation for National and Community Service, 1201 New York Avenue, NW, Washington, D.C. 20525.

✧ Your public library has good sources of information on state and private financial aid sources.

✧ Many foundations offer programs to help pay the cost of college education. If you are a member of a labor union, you'll want to see if they offer financial aid.

✧ Check with local service organizations, such as Rotary, Elks, and Lions.

✧ Be sure to look at organizations connected with your child's field of interest; e.g., your state teachers association, engineering associations, state and federal bar associations, and the American Medical Association. Your public library will have various directories.

✧ If you or your spouse is a veteran, don't overlook their

services. Contact the Veterans' Affairs officer in your county.

If your child is a good student who is motivated and has the desire and drive, there is help. No college wants your child to be unsuccessful. Colleges do a much better job of helping students than they did a generation ago. It is not necessary to complain. Get in there and do some homework early, while your child is still in high school.

Another excellent source of help is the publication, *Cap and Gown*, published by Key Corp. Call their hotline, 1-800-KEY-LEND, Monday through Friday, 8 a.m. to 4:30 p.m. Or write Key Corp., 5000 Tideman Road, Cleveland, OH 44144.

Also, try the Federal Student Aid Information Center, P.O. Box 84, Washington, DC 20044-0084. The guide is free or is available on-line on the Department of Education's World Wide Web site (http/www.ed.gov).

Most colleges have a scholarship handbook put out by the office of academic affairs. It lists all scholarships and grants available to their students.

HOW YOUR CHILD CAN BE ADMITTED TO COLLEGE

Some small colleges are recognizing that some students do not do well on the Scholastic Assessment Test (SAT)—even some first-generation college students with high grade-point averages. Students are now allowed to submit writing samples and interview with college staff. High school grades may reveal more about a student's success in college than math and verbal skills scores on a test. There is more than one kind of intelligence, and it is difficult to measure *desire* to succeed.

Very few major four-year colleges allow students to avoid the SAT. Most of the colleges having that option are smaller liberal arts colleges. Most two-year state community colleges will accept students without SAT scores. The costs at community colleges are less, and some classes are free to some students. Community colleges just might be the answer to a student who can't get into a four-year college. At a small college, the student can get more individual help. A student can always transfer to a large four-year college later.

To write the essay for your college of choice, you will need to get *Do It Write* by G. Gary Ripple, Ph.D (Octameron Associates, P.O. Box 2748, Alexandria, VA 22302, 703-836-5480, $4). This 32-page booklet explains how you can write winning essays that will stand out from the others, as the admission committee sifts through thousands of applications.

Writing Your College Application Essay by Sarah Myers McGinty (College Board Publications, Box 886, New York, NY 10101, $9.95) will help students write distinctive college application essays. The college will be looking at each student's essay to find out who they are and how they write.

Here are some pointers that college admissions officers offer:

* Stay in your own state if you are considering a public college. Nonresidents usually face stiffer academic requirements than in-state students.
* Admissions officers are paying special attention to recommendations from teachers, interviews, application essays, and unusual backgrounds.
* Students who are masters of one particular area are more attractive; e.g., a student who has focused on business in high school, or a student who made wise investments in the stock market. One freshman I know has $4,000 invested in the stock market. He can tell you all the good

companies. He reads the *Wall Street Journal*. His dad is a regular investor in the stock market, and the student is excellent at math. He is not the greatest student, but he could be admitted into a college specializing in business.

✳ Colleges are looking for students with the entrepreneurial spirit—the kind of student willing to take something on and see it through, one with a vision who is willing to take a risk. This could be kid with a paper route who increased the number of subscriptions by 25% and then saved part of his money for college, or the girl who baby-sat since fourth grade and used part of her earnings to buy stocks under her father's advice. When it came time for college, she had several thousand dollars in stocks earning money for her. Colleges are looking for young people who plan ahead.

✳ When students write their essay to the admissions office, they should be sure to point out their personal strengths. They may have a special skill in making and keeping friends. They may be class leaders. One girl in a small school in eastern Oregon read every book in her school. The college of your child's choice may accept him because of a unique talent. SAT scores are only one indicator of potential success as a student. Desire may be the deciding factor.

✳ Admissions officers will certainly look for students who have overcome hardships, such as the student who maintained average grades and worked six hours a day at a filling station during high school to help support his mother and two younger siblings. With the help of a high school teacher, he received a scholarship that paid all four years at a university. He's still working six hours a day and is sending money home to help support his family. He has proven that he is responsible, has courage, is resourceful, has great empathy, is generous, and has many friends. The admissions officers know he will be a successful student, because he has proven his abilities and his willingness to learn.

* Colleges are always looking for students who are willing to get involved in community projects. One student was admitted to a small college, based on her willingness to spend Saturday mornings at the local nursing home helping make life a little bit better for some older folks who were delighted with her kindness and friendliness. The nursing home director wrote her a letter of recommendation which got her into the school of her choice.

* If a student has a strong faith and has been involved in his church, then perhaps a sectarian college might be the right one for him. There is always a need for people to serve in some area of ministry that helps others develop their faith. These are the kind of students who demonstrate leadership in their school, community, and church.

* One rigorous academic small college took a student with B and C grades who asked the college what he could learn there. He wanted to know if a particular subject was taught and why they taught a certain way. The student showed he was willing to take risks and was very curious, with a strong desire to learn.

* Motivation and desire is the most important factor for some colleges that require a lot of independent study. One admissions officer indicated that they go more on student essays, recommendations, and interviews. They are looking for students who keep their appointments and are organized.

* Early admission policy might help your student get into his college of first choice. Students should be sure to outline concrete reasons why they want to attend a certain college. They are not interested in comments such as "I would love to attend your college because I have an aunt who lives there."

✳ Personality will play a major factor. Honesty, friendliness, self-reliance, resourcefulness, kindness, and courage are all characteristics that will help a student be successful. Admissions officers are apt to ask questions, such as "What do you do on weekends or on your time off? What are your hobbies?"

✳ Students need to be able to communicate, both verbally and in writing. If a student is weak in these two areas, you might consider getting a tutor in the early part of high school.

SO YOUR CHILD HAS A HANDICAPPING CONDITION

Don't panic. There's a college for your child. During your child's junior year in high school, talk with your high school career counselor and ask if they have the latest edition of Directory of College Facilities and Services for People With Disabilities by Carol H. Thomas and James L. Thomas (The Oryx Press, 4041 N. Central at Indian School Road, Phoenix, AZ 85012, 602-265-2651, $125).

If it is not available at the school, go to your nearest college or university and make good use of it. The publication lists colleges by state and handicapping condition they are able to serve. You will be able to select the appropriate college that can best serve your child. For example, Eastern Oregon State College at La Grande, Oregon, will accept students who are visually impaired/blind, hearing impaired/deaf, speech/language impaired, orthopedically or mobility impaired, or who have learning disabilities or developmental disabilities. It lists how many students are in each program.

The publication has a listing of grants, ranging from $10,000 to $50,000, available to students with specific learning disabilities. This is a very comprehensive publication because it lists 1600 colleges and universities in the U.S. and its territories and Canada.

In 1975, Congress passed the Public Law 94-142. The Education Act for Children With a Handicapping Condition states that "a free and appropriate education be provided in the least restrictive environment" to all handicapped children between the ages of 3 and 21. Latest figures indicate that nearly 12 percent or 1.4 million students are in training past high school with at least one disability. Federal law also states that "no otherwise qualified handicapped individual in the U.S. ... shall, solely by reason of his handicap, be excluded from participating in, be excluded from the benefits of or be subjected to discrimination under any program or activity receiving federal financial assistance."

Most colleges do provide for handicapping conditions. Some colleges provide greater opportunities than others. You need to be informed. Do your homework before your child's sophomore year in high school. There are lots of good resources available.

BIBLIOGRAPHY

Chapter 4-5 Books

BOOKS FOR YOUR BABY'S SHELF

Yes, babies come equipped, ready and willing to be read to. They learn with their senses. Simple books are available that babies can taste without shredding. A baby's brain is like a computer. It stores information to be used later. Reading increases a baby's future vocabulary and increases future language ability. Your baby will enjoy listening to you read to an older child. An older child will enjoy reading to her baby sibling. Try some of these:

Baby's First Words by Lars Wik. Random House, 1985. This cardboard book of photos features familiar objects and actions in the child's world.
Mother Goose by Gyo Fujikama. Platt and Munk, 1981. A popular artist fills this big book with his typical happy children.
Eye Winker, Tom Tinker, Chin Chopper: 50 Musical Fingerplays by Tom Glazer. Zephyr, 1973. The best of the finger play books, this is a collection of old favorites and new games that are easy to learn and fun to do.
The Me Book by John E. Johnson. Random House, 1984. A soft, safe nontoxic tubable cloth book with the popular dog Spot pictured with his toys on every page. Also, *Sweet Dreams, Spot.*
The Lullaby Song, edited by Jane Yolen. Illustrated by Charles Mikolaycak. Harcourt Brace Jovanovich, 1986. A collection of soothing lullabies sing a child to sleep, offering sweet dreams and security in this collection of beloved favorites from around the world.
What Is It? by Toma Hobon. Green Willow, 1983. Handsome photos of familiar objects baby will recognize.

BOOKS AND YOUR TODDLER

Reading material for toddlers should include books and magazines with large, clear, realistic pictures. Avoid picture books that are too abstract for your child to "read" visually. Cluttered pages with lots of action may be too busy for your toddler.

You don't need books with a lot of plot. You want books that name things. Objects should be sorted into meaningful categories. Books for toddlers should be made of durable materials. Books that are delicate should be put out of reach of little hands for now.

Toddlers will also enjoy sitting in your lap and looking at real objects in catalogs. Remember, they are learning to talk and will enjoy naming objects.

You can read aloud to your toddler while she is playing, as well as at bedtime. She will also enjoy listening to the lullaby that you sang when she was younger. Read as often as your toddler wants. This is an excellent time to get your child hooked on books.

Check your local public library for wordless books that are just right for the toddler to look at.

Early Words by Richard Scarry. Random House, 1976. This sturdy book with

SUCCESS STARTS EARLY!

Frannie the bunny can be shared by the two of you.
Goodnight Moon by Margaret Wise Brown. Harper and Row, 1947. It is about a
   child's desire for power of her own. This classic will be around awhile longer.
Marmalade's Nap by Cindy Wheeler. Knopf, 1983. Delightfully simple story
   about a little cat's need for a nap.
Pat the Bunny by Dorothy Kunhardt. Golden, 1962. A classic with a variety of
   textures glued into place for making firsthand connections between words
   and touch.
Sam Who Never Forgets by Eye Rice. Puffin, 1980. Sam the zookeeper feeds all
   the animals and never forgets. Older toddlers will enjoy the surprise and
   repetition.
Shopping Trip by Helen Oxenbury. Dial 1982. With simplicity, charm, and humor,
   a young toddler goes shopping for shoes, then to the grocery store, and a
   restaurant.
Taste the Raindrops by Anna Hines. Green Willow, 1983. A tale about a child who
   longs to go out in the rain. Full of language and a happy ending.
The Very Hungry Caterpillar by Eric Carle. Philomel, 1969. From tiny eggs to
   beautiful butterfly, the story of a tiny caterpillar as it eats its way through the
   week. Brilliant paintings.
Where's My Baby? by H.A. Rey. Houghton Mifflin, 1943. A mother and baby
   animal book. Every toddler should own this classic.
Where's Spot? by Eric Hill. Putnam, 1980. The dog Spot is lost and hasn't eaten
   his dinner in this peek-a-boo game of opening flaps on every page until Spot
   is at last found.

BOOKS FOR THREE- AND FOUR-YEAR-OLDS

Three- and four-year-olds are emerging from the frustration of their own
inabilities. They are still struggling to gain mastery over their physical skills and
developing competence in verbal communications. They are able to use language
to express most of their needs, emotions, and ideas. They are able to run, jump, spin,
and climb more freely.
   Children this age will enjoy picture books about independence, imaginary friends, scary stories—real and unreal—fairytales, folktales, and fantasy.
They enjoy stories with simple plots. They want to know about themselves when
they were babies, as well as about relatives and extended family. This is a time to
read stories about friends, such as *Best Friends* by Miriam Cohen. They'll enjoy
the plot in wordless books. The illustrations carry the plot. While the family is
having "read-at-home time," your three- to four-year-old will enjoy "reading"
wordless books.
   Books for this age are numerous and fun to read aloud. If read to two or
three times daily, they will probably learn to read on their own. Now that's exciting
parent and child.
   Here are ten books every thre- and four-year-old should know:

The Carrot Seed by Ruth Krauss. Harper and Row, 1945. This classic about the
   determined little planter will be read many times.
Curious George by H. A. Rey. Houghton Mifflin, 1941. This classic has delighted
   children with his scary situations, from which he is always rescued by "the
   man in the yellow hat."
Freight Train by Donald Crews. Green Willow, 1984. It's always fun to watch
   freight trains go by. You'll want to count the cars.
Gilberto and the Wind by Marie Hall. Viking, 1963. Don't let your child fail to

213

experience this book about a boy and the wind—how it sounds, what it blows, what it breaks, and what a little boy can do with it.

The Little Red Hen. Clarion Books, 1973. The irresistible pictures and an old tale are just right to please threes and fours.

Make Way for Ducklings by Robert McCloskey. Viking, 1941. Children of all ages will enjoy the ducklings and their mother crossing the street with the help of a policeman.

May I Bring a Friend? by Beatrice Schenk de Regniers. Atheneum, 1964. This wonderful read-aloud book will delight children from three and up, as the animals are welcomed to tea by the king and queen.

Poems to Read to the Very Young, selected by Josette Frank. Random House, 1982. These well-selected poems have been a favorite for a long time.

The Snowy Day by Ezra Jack Keats. Viking, 1962. The simple words and glowing pictures tell of a little boy's fun in the snow.

The Tale of Peter Rabbit by Beatrix Potter. Warne, 1902. This classic is about savoring power and independence. For all children who love a little suspense and danger.

BOOKS FOR FIVE-YEAR-OLDS

When selecting books for your five-year-old, the text can be longer and language less simple. The attention spans of fives are growing like the rest of them. So they can sit still longer and deal with a more complex story.

Your goal should be developing a love of books and reading. When your child grows up with a rich diet of wonderful books, the appetite for learning to read falls into place. Naturally, rather than having to be hammered in by others, learning to read should be easy. It will be if you read to your five-year-old as often as she wants to be read to.

Your five-year-old will enjoy fantasy (such as *Ramona the Pest* or *Fredrick's Fables*), books about animals, big things that go (such as *Little Toot*), and stories without books (your tales of when your were little).

They begin to get the idea that we read a book from left to right. They'll tell about the picture. All you need to do is read the text, then let him/her tell about the picture.

Many five-year-olds will be reading before they start to school in the first grade. By reading and discussing stories, learning to read should be an easy task—as easy as learning to talk and .walk. It almost becomes a natural thing to do. You will also want your child seeing you reading and enjoying a book.

Here are nine books every five-year-old should know:

Bedtime for Francis by Russel Hoban. Harper and Row, 1960. This book has become a classic. Francis the badger is in bed singing the alphabet, until she gets to "T." Kids will identify with the little badger's problem.

Caps for Sale by Esphyr Slobodkina. Addison-Wesley, 1947. This classic will be loved by children, especially the repetition and power of telling those monkey-see-monkey-do thieves to "give me back my cap!"

The Little Engine That Could by Watty Piper. Buccaneer Books, 1981. This classic tale of determination and belief in oneself first came out in the thirties.

Mike Mulligan and His Steam Shovel by Virginia Lee Barton. Houghton Mifflin, 1939. A meaningful tale about faithful friends and about "new" not necessarily being best.

Millions of Cats by Wanda Gag. Coward, McCann, 1928. This classic folktale is the story of a very old man who set out to look for one sweet fluffy feline and returned with "hundreds of cats."

Nutshell Library by Maurice Sendak. Harper and Row, 1962. This book contains four gems: *Chicken Soup and Rice, One Was Johnny, Pierre, and Alligators All Around.* You'll find a counting book, alphabet book, a moral tale, and a romp through the seasons.

The Runaway Bunny by Margaret Wise Brown. Harper and Row, 1942. A tender-loving tale of a little bunny who dreams of runaway adventure and a loving mom who reassures her runaway that she'll never be far away.

Stone Soup by Marcia Brown. Scribners, 1947. This classic tale about three hungry soldiers and how they made soup with three stones plus a dash of cunning and humor. You could make stone soup for dinner. The ingredients are in the book.

The Story About Ping by Marjorie Flack. Penguin, 1977. Five-year-olds can easily relate to this tale about a duck that does not want to get spanked for being the last one home.

BOOKS FOR SIX- AND SEVEN-YEAR-OLDS

Books for sixes and sevens take on a new dimension. These are the years when children get started with the formal business of learning to read. It is also the time when most parents stop reading to their kids. This is a time when you'll want to listen to your child read and then continue to read stories a year or so above their reading ability. Their listening comprehension is at least two years above their reading ability. Easy-to-read books begin to lose their appeal at a time when they have a rich need for listening to good children's literature.

Their ability to understand complex plots goes well beyond their word-attack skills. You can provide them with easy-to-read books, but they also need challenging books to grow into. They will enjoy "rereading" the books you read during the fives. They may read them over and over.

Reading for six- and seven-year-olds is a bridge to understanding that other people have problems, feelings, and experiences like their own. A good story invites the children to step outside themselves into someone else's shoes for awhile. Kids at this age experience a wide range of feelings, and they can begin to understand them through good literature.

They enjoy books about independence and interdependence, such as *Where the Wild Things Are.* Max is on his own, he faces the unknown. Kids enjoy books about family and independence in the family, such as *Alexander and the Terrible, Horrible, No Good, Very Bad Day*, in which Alexander begins to understand that everyone has days in which nothing goes right.

They can handle books about dealing with siblings, as in *Worse Than Willy*, in which two siblings complain to their grandpa about their new baby brother.

They relish humor and usually have a firm fix on fantasy and reality. They enjoy two green monsters tiptoeing into a bedroom, as in *Pleasant Dreams*. They love to hear folktales, both old and new. My grandkids always enjoyed my telling them stores about life when I was a boy their age. They love fairytales of all sorts—stories like those in *The Big Golden Book of Fairytales*. Then there are those wonderful wordless books, like *The Mystery of the Giant Foot Print*.

They want to read and hear books about real things, too, like in *Dinosaur Time*. Then there are the concept books, such as *Trucks You Can Count On*.

This is not a time to quit reading aloud to your children. These read-aloud sessions might include a younger sibling or an older one. I read *Charlotte's Web* to my second-grade grandson, and his fifth-grade brother listened in and enjoyed it. I can recall listening to *Gone With the Wind* being read to my 12- and 14-year-old brothers. It was always a happy time to hear my mother's reading voice.

Here are ten books every six- and seven-year-old should know:

Alexander and the Terrible, Horrible, No Good, Very Bad Day by Judith Viorst. Atheneum, 1972. Everyone has days when nothing goes right, when you wish you had stayed in bed—or left for Australia. Alexander's complaints are both recognizable and laughable.

Amos and Boris by William Steig. Penguin, 1977. This is a perfect match for six- and seven-year-olds about Amos the mouse and Boris the whale, who are the closest of friends.

The Fairy Tale Treasure by Virginia Haviland. Conrad, McCann, 1972. One of the best collections of old favorites for this age group.

Frog and Toad Are Friends by Arnold Lobel. Harper and Row, 1970. In an easy-to-read format, these short stories about two loyal friends can be enjoyed as read-aloud. They're right on target in feelings. Also, *Frog and Toad Together, Frog and Toad All Year*, and *Days with Frog and Toad.*

Go, Dog, Go by P. D. Eastman. Random House, 1961. Action-packed dogs with plenty of zany humor to add story to limited text.

The House at Pooh Corner by A. A. Milne. Dutton, 1961. This is a great read-aloud story with rich language. Great pen and ink illustrations, too.

Ramona the Pest by Beverly Cleary. Morrow, 1968. Ramona is in kindergarten and is having trouble with the teacher and a classmate on how things are "'sposed" to be. Also, *Ramona the Brave* and others.

The Snowman by Raymond Briggs. Random House, 1978. This exquisite fantasy about a boy and his snowman who take off on a thrilling adventure is the stuff snowflakes and daydreams are made of.

Steve by John Steptoe. Harper and Row, 1969. This is a touching story of Little Steve who lives with another family. Robert, an only child, is bothered by Steve and "his old spoiled self."

Where the Wild Things Are by Maurice Sendak. Harper and Row, 1963. When Max, who's been acting like a "wild thing," is sent to bed without supper, he takes off on an adventure that leads to a special place where he becomes king.

The Cricket in Times Square by George Selden. Straus and Giroux, 1960. It all begins when Chester, a cricket from Connecticut, gets whisked off in a picnic basket and finds himself in Times Square Subway Station. This is a story of friendship, cooperation and a taste of fame. A treat for the whole family.

Dominic by William Steig. Straus and Giroux, 1972. This is a wonderful story about courage and imagination along life's highway. The ever-present danger of the Doomsday Robbers awaits, but Dominic, the young hero, is around with a magic spear that helps him carve out his own identity.

BOOKS FOR EIGHT- AND NINE-YEAR-OLDS

Selecting books for this age is more challenging, as it calls for more individual attention than ever before. Their range of reading ability and interest is varied. Some eight-year-olds may be avid readers, while some are still breaking the reading code. Some will want to read the novel on your bedside table.

By now, the world of school has become routine. They want to live up to their own and adults' expectations. They will read books about group life and how differences affect them. They may enjoy *The Hundred Dresses*, which is about fitting in and being ostracized.

Much of their life centers on friends and school. Children's relationship in the family is also reflected in realistic fiction. All the newest family arrangements can be found in books for this age group, such as *Tales of a Fourth Grade Nothing*.

Because these kids are developing a growing interest in the past, they will focus on history, fact or fiction. They want to know how kids played, worked, and lived in the distant past, as in The Little House series.

Mysteries hold a special appeal for eight- and nine-year-olds. They are into chapter books. A good reader will gobble them up like peanuts at a ballgame. Fortunately, writers and publishers recognize the popularity of the mystery genre and have published many books to satisfy their taste.

This age group is attracted to books about fantasy with plenty of humor. That's why *Charlotte's Web* is such a big hit.

Folktales and fairytales offer another route to fantasy and adventure. Now that they are secure in their understanding of real and make-believe, the world of once-upon-a-time provides a splendid realm in which they can find safe thrills in witches, dragons, and the unknown (try *Mean Jake and the Devil*). They will laugh out loud at these devilish tales.

They still love picture books for the older reader. Some of the picture books they like tend to be longer and more involved. *The Country Bunny and the Little Golden Shoes* is a good example. Some of them will even go back and reread some of the picture books you read aloud.

They are into information books, such as atlases, Guiness Book of Records, true baseball stories, UFO's, and science-related texts. Some books on poetry will appeal to them. If you read poetry to your children early, then they will enjoy the rhymes in poetry books.

Here are ten books every eight- and nine-year-old should know:

Bunnicula by Deborah and James Howe. Athenium, 1979. Told by Harold, "a dog by profession," this is a mystery-comedy about a bunny found in a movie theater, where Dracula was playing. Good suspense and humor for family read-aloud time. Also, *The Further Adventures of Bunnicula* and *The Celery Stalks at Midnight*.

Charlotte's Web by E. B. White. Harper and Row, 1952. A beloved story about a spider and a pig. It has everything children relish, such as suspense, humor, friendship, and adventure. This is a gem everyone in the family can enjoy.

Freckle Juice by Judy Blume. Four Winds, 1971. Andrew wanted freckles like his classmate Nick. He is so eager that he pays Sharon 50 cents for a secret recipe. This books is about a foolish desire to conform.

The Garden of Abdul Gasazi by Chris Van Allsburg. Houghton Mifflin, 1979. Alan is left to care for miss Hester's bad-mannered dog, Fritz. His trouble begins when Fritz bolts through the entrance to the forbidden garden of the magician Abdul Gasazi.

Little House Series by Laura Ingalls Wilder. Harper and Row, 1935. This is the classic series of the Ingalls family's move west and life on the frontier with its danger, hardship, and adventure. There are seven volumes in the series that appeared on television of the years.

No One Is Going to Nashville by Mavis Jakes. Knap, 1983. Sonia's relationship with her father and stepmother is so warmly real that all three characters seem to leap into life in a story that is a refreshing tonic.

Ramona Quimby Age 8 by Beverly Cleary. Independent Ramona runs into a lot of problems trying to cope with a new school, her parents' busy schedules, and a misunderstanding with her teacher. Also, Ramona the Pest, Ramona and Her Father, and Henry and the Clubhouse.

Sarah, Plain and Tall by Patricia MacLachlan. Harper and Row, 1985. Two

motherless children and their father advertise for a wife and mother. What
they get is Sarah, plain and tall, but possessed of a beauty all her own. A
wonderful moving story set in the 1800s.

BOOKS FOR TEN- TO TWELVE-YEAR-OLDS

Reading aloud to this age should be continued, as it is a great idea at every
age. Sometimes, independent reading seems to be falling off. If you enjoy it, your
children will enjoy it at almost any age. If you read to your 10- to 12-year-old,
younger siblings will no doubt be listening in. Make reading aloud a lifelong
custom in your home.

The Read-Aloud Handbook by Jim Trelease is an excellent source of
books to read to children, ages toddler and up. It is well worth the $12.95. Most of
the books listed for children are available in public libraries.

Here are 10 books every 10- to 12-year-old should know:

Are You There, God? It's Me by Judy Blume. Bradbury, 1970. Margaret is a typical
suburban 11-year-old, neither bizarre nor tragic. Her concerns are, quite
simply, with growing up. She is re-evaluating loyalty, empathy, and family
feelings.

The Book of Three (The Prydain Chronicles) by Lloyd Alexander. Holt, 1964. This
fantasy, based on Welsh legend, pits the boy Taran, assistant pigkeeper,
against an array of villains equalling those in any Steven Spielberg flick.
Others include *The Prydain Chronicles, Black Cauldron, Westmark,* and
Time Cat.

Bridge to Terabithia by Katherine Paterson. Crowell, 1977. Leslie and Jess are
from different backgrounds, but they form a close friendship and create an
imaginary secret kingdom.

Island of the Blue Dolphins by Scott O'Dell. Houghton Miffline, 1960. This book
is based on the true experience of a young woman in the 1800s. Karana, the
girl, is a native of the islands off the coast of California. There's an almost
mythical quality to Karana's lonely "walkabout."

The Lion, the Witch, and the Wardrobe by C. S. Lewis. Macmillan, 1951. Four
English children step through a magical wardrobe into the enchanted land of
Narnia, where they meet the lion king Aslan and a wicked white witch, who
manages to delude one of their band into thinking she is on their side. Good
for reading aloud as a family.

Alice's Adventure in Wonderland by Lewis Carroll. St. Martin's, 1977. Some
regard Alice as an acquired taste. Children at this age are mature enough to
appreciate some of the satire and humor.

My Side of the Mountain by Jean George. Dutton, 1959. Teenager Sam Gribley is
looking for his roots on the farm abandoned by his forebears. He is determined
to live out a year on his ancestral acres as a mountain boy.

Roll of Thunder, Hear My Cry by Mildren Taylor. Dial, 1976. This truthful book
by a black author is about the struggles that a black girl has in Mississippi
during the depression. Cassie and her brothers retain their integrity and grow
up independent.

Tuck Everlasting by Natalie Babbitt. Farrar, Straus and Giroux, 1975. This gem
should be enjoyed by everyone in the family. Winnie Foster lives at the edge
of an ancient wood. The land has been owned by the Foster family for several
generations, but it does not know about the great oak tree and the secret that
lies in the spring bubbling up from its roots.

A Wrinkle in Time by Madeline L'Engle. Farrer, Straus and Giroux, 1962. Two children search for their missing scientist fathers in a time warp and are subjected to great danger. The dialogue is superb. The humor and the rich weave of plot make this a timeless wonder of a book.

CLASSICS THAT EVERY CHILD SHOULD KNOW:

Androcles and the Lion from Aesop's Fables.
The Adventures of the Windmill by Miguel de Cevantes.
The Early Days of Black Beauty by Ann Sewell.
The Golden Touch, adapted by Nathaniel Hawthorne.
Gulliver's Travels by Jonathon Swift.
How Arthur Was Crowned King by Sir Thomas Malory.
Robin Hood and the Merry Little Old Woman by Eva March Tappen.
The Ugly Duckling by Hans Christen Anderson.
Ulysses and the Cyclops by Homer
Every child age eight and up should hear these classical poems:
Casey at the Bat by Ernest Lawrence Thayer.
The Charge of the Light Brigade by Alfred Lord Tennyson.
For all ages:
It Couldn't Be Done by Edgar A. Guest.
The Highwayman by Alfred Noyes.
Paul Revere's Ride by Henry Wadsworth.
Classics to read aloud to kids age 8 and up:
"Jim Baker's Bluejay Yarn," from *A Tramp Aboard* by Mark Twain.
"The Glorious Whitewasher" from *The Adventures of Tom Sawyer*
    by Mark Twain.
The Ransom of Red Chief by O. Henry.
Rip Van Winkle by Washington Irving.
Romeo and Juliet by William Shakespeare.
Classics to read aloud to kids age 11 and up:
The Adventures of Huckleberry Finn by Mark Twain.
The Adventures of the Speckled Bond by Sir Arthur Conan Doyle.
The Call of the Wild by Jack London.
The Red Badge of Courage by Stephen Crane.

HOLIDAY STORIES:

A Visit from Old St. Nicholas: by Clement Clarke Moore.
A Christmas Carol by Charles Dickens.
The Risen Lord, as retold by William Canton.
Ezra's Thanksgiving Out West by Eugene Field.
The Gift of the Magi by O. Henry.
The Legend of Sleepy Hollow by Washington Irving.
Pharoah of the Hard Heart, as retold by William Canton.

Chapter 10-11 Books

Here are some children's books for about careers and work ethics:

Leave the Cooking to Me by Judie Angell (Bantam Doubleday Dell, 1990). A
    teenage girl proves to herself and her mother that she can do something on her

own by building a successful summer catering business. This humorous story will be enjoyed by most girls. Ages 10-14.

El Chino by Allen Say (Houghton Mifflin Co., 1990). Color illustrations by the author. A young Chinese-American man, defeated by his lack of height in his desire to play professional basketball manages to become the world's first Chinese bullfighter. A true story. Ages 6-9.

Pig Pig Gets a Job by David McPhail. (Dutton Children's books, 1990) Color illustrations by the author. A young pig who wants spending money fantasizes about the grown-up work he could do. This funny, well-illustrated book could inspire good discussion on allowances and chores. Ages 4-8.

Billy Boone by Alison Smith (Charles Scribner's Sons, 1989). A determined girl sets out to learn the trumpet, although it is considered a "male" instrument, and her equally spunky grandmother helps her persevere. Young readers will be intrigued by the characters and will find much for discussion. Ages 9-12.

Bet You Can't by Penny Dale (J. B. Lippincott Co., 1988) Color illustrations by the author. Siblings make a game of bedtime cleanup in this simple but effective story about cooperation in work. An excellent read-aloud book. Ages 3-5.

My War With Goggle-Eyes by Anne Fine (Joy Street Books, 1989). A girl feels threatened by her mother's new boyfriend until she realizes the man has good qualities and values that bring happiness and stability to her family. Kitty's attitude changes gradually and naturally. Ages 8-12.

Christina Katerina and the Time She Quit the Family by Patricia Lee Gauch (Putnam & Grosset Group, Inc., 1987). Color illustrations by Elise Primavera. Agnes learns what it means to pick up her own mess and figures out how to wind yarn by herself and tuck herself into bed. Great read-aloud tale. Ages 4-7.

SUCCESS STARTS EARLY!

ANOTHER EDUCATIONAL TITLE
FROM BLUE BIRD PUBLISHING

ISBN 0-933025-47-5
$12.95   4th edition

This homeschool classic has been reviewed by
*Booklist, Library Journal, Home Education Magazine,
New Big Book of Home Learning*, and many more.

Available at bookstores and libraries.

SUCCESS STARTS EARLY!

ANOTHER EDUCATIONAL TITLE
FROM BLUE BIRD PUBLISHING

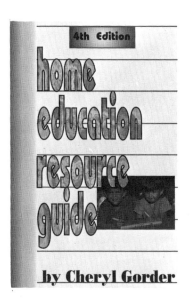

ISBN 0-933025-48-3
$12.95   4th edition

A homeschooling bestseller!

"If you can afford only one resource directory,
this is the one to buy."—Library Journal.

Available at bookstores and libraries.

SUCCESS STARTS EARLY!

ANOTHER EDUCATIONAL TITLE
FROM BLUE BIRD PUBLISHING

ISBN 0-933025-17-3
$15.95   4th edition

This program has been adopted by many Literacy Groups and Right-to-Read Groups Across the United States and Canada.

"I absolutely love this book!"
—Carol Sanford, literacy volunteer.

Available at bookstores and libraries.

Success Starts Early!

OTHER TITLES FROM BLUE BIRD PUBLISHING

Available in bookstores and libraries.

Home Schools: An Alternative (4th ed) **$12.95**
A home schooling bestseller.
Home Education Resource Guide (4th e.) **$12.95**
A home schooling bestseller.
Heartful Parenting **$14.95**
Discover the secret ingredient to successful parenting.
Dr. Christman's Learn-to-Read Book **$15.95**
Phonics program for all ages. Adopted by many
literacy and right-to-read groups
Kindergarten at Home **$22.95**
An interactive kindergarten curriculum for
homeschoolers. Useful activities for teachers too.
Countdown to College **$14.95**
Recommended by the Educational Assistance
Council for parents of high school seniors.
Kids First! Family Education Program **$12.95**
Gets parents involved in their child's education.

More titles available on parenting & education.
Full catalog on Web Site: www.bluebird1.com

Blue Bird Publishing
2266 S. Dobson #275
Mesa AZ 85202
(602) 831-6063 FAX (602) 831-1829
Email: bluebird@bluebird1.com
Web Site: www.bluebird1.com